T0383453

Barbara Kasten

Barbara Kasten

Architecture & Film (2015–2020)

edited by Stephanie Cristello

Cover
Still from *Sideways* (2015/2020).
Courtesy of the artist

Design
Anna Cattaneo

Editorial coordination
Emma Cavazzini

Copy editing
Andrew Ellis

Layout
Paola Ranzini Pallavicini

First published in Italy in 2022 by
Skira editore S.p.A.
Palazzo Casati Stampa
via Torino 61
20123 Milano
Italy

Printed and bound in Italy. First edition

ISBN: 978-88-572-4719-9

Distributed in USA, Canada, Central
& South America by ARTBOOK | D.A.P.
75, Broad Street Suite 630, New York,
NY 10004, USA.
Distributed elsewhere in the world
by Thames and Hudson Ltd.
181A High Holborn, London WC1V 7QX,
United Kingdom.

www.skira.net

Contents

What Light Does:
The Architecture & Film of Barbara Kasten

Stephanie Cristello

"I am not photographing light;
I am photographing what light does."[1]
Barbara Kasten

In the work of artist Barbara Kasten (b. 1936, Chicago), the camera figured into her early practice insofar as it could document ephemeral abstractions of light and shadow cast upon the walls of her studio. They are photographs that capture images in space through the means of recording. Once the light was cut, the work too ceased to exist, yet the translation of the experience remained in circulation. Then as now, the structures conceived within Kasten's studio did not function as only stages or props, but rather as sites for living— the photograph merely a record of that life. To understand Kasten's singular and innovative contributions to the nature of abstraction as a conceptual artist, we must see beyond the record.

To photograph light is to elevate one instance of experience beyond all others, to make static what is never still, to halt time and break how phenomena relate to one another. Paradoxically, to make an image of what light does, to show how it behaves, is to acknowledge its inherent and necessary dynamism. The material of Kasten's work, light itself, unfolds against our everyday awareness of its movement; as keeper of time, an ever-changing process of illumination, an act of "obliscence."[2] This term, a moment that refers to a theory of memory by which a being experiences experience, defines the beginning of a sequence that progresses from involvement, remembrance, and ultimately, to forgetting. Across her work, it is the latter she suspends.

Kasten's experiments of light in space—through measured construction, manipulation, and control—inflect what we already know of this source whose cycles constitute the basis of life. In the studio as much as in any environment, the question of what light does is a matter of perception. It asks *how we see* through a manifestation of the conditions that create an image or experience. Light informs our understanding of the world and our place within it. For over five decades, this formulation of light-as-material permeates Kasten's work, which has spanned the traditional genres of photography, painting, sculpture, installation, textile, theater, and performance, in service of her phenomenological project. Across her conceptual output, her recent investigations into architecture and film provide a fertile return to the ethos of her artistic approach—one that is rooted in placing us as an active participant in an environment that shapes and is shaped by us.

The premise of this book spans five years of Kasten's recent installations and exhibitions following *Barbara Kasten: Stages*, the artist's first major museum survey at the Institute of Contemporary Art in Philadelphia, followed by the Graham Foundation in Chicago in partnership with the Chicago Architecture Biennial, and MOCA Pacific Design Center in Los Angeles (2016). Post *Stages*, we enter a period of unparalleled energy in Kasten's oeuvre through distinct avenues that open amid each of the author's contributions. With a specific focus on architecture and film, whose fields allow for an enriched and expanded conversation surrounding Kasten's work beyond the photographic, the texts reach back to incorporate elements of her practice since the 1970s, that anticipate her current installations, alongside unearthed comparisons and histories. Certain momentous encounters, including Kasten's *Artist/City* (*Crown Hall*) (2018) installed within Mies van der Rohe's iconic glass and steel structure and her solo exhibition *Scenarios* (2020–21) at the Aspen Art Museum, serve as a primer to access her revolutionary methods of abstraction.

The duration of this phase (2015–20) in Kasten's work is as much a subject as duration itself. Across essays and interviews by Hans Ulrich Obrist, Humberto Moro, Mimi Zeiger, and myself, the phenomenology of abstraction as an invention of light, atmosphere, form, and time in Kasten's site-specific installations and films are revealed their attention to her ritualistic practice as both a spiritual and perceptual endeavor. As Don DeLillo writes in *The Body Artist*, time becomes something more like itself, "sheer and bare, empty of shelter"[3] as we enter the architectural traces that Kasten imparts. Her approach to form in recent work establishes incidences of light that modulate our expectations of space in service of new concrete experiences. While the original performance in Kasten's creation of her environments often remains unseen in the final work, signs of her movement persist as something you look through, are touched by, and inhabit. The last five years of Kasten's commissions unfold as speculative conversations with architecture, among them buildings by Mies and Shigeru Ban, instilled through a Bauhaus approach that dissolves the hierarchical division between artist and viewer, architect and artist. These recent exhibitions and projects point to a shift in Kasten's work—from the need of immediacy via a camera to capture a scene, to the embrace of a stretching of time and space that forms an image—allowing our eyes the power of a lens, transforming our bodies in service of perception in collaboration with the built environment.

In Kasten's in-depth interview with Obrist, commissioned here following significant collaborations, among them the design of the stage for Obrist's *Interview Marathon* in Chicago[4] (2018) and their inclusion in the film *The New Bauhaus*[5] (2019) on artist László Moholy-Nagy, the artist speaks of her early inspirations from the Bauhaus (as a student of member Trude Guermonprez) and Modernist architecture. In *Towards an Emotional Architecture*, Humberto Moro's interwoven comparison to the sensitivities of space in the buildings of Mexican architect Luis Barragán allows for a lengthened consideration of Kasten's treatment of light, geometry, and color in both two and three dimensions—from the seminal *Construct* (1979–86) series to the recent *Progression* (2017–ongoing) works. My essay, *On Goddesses and Sacred Sites*, presents an elective history of scenes in relation to Kasten through her early cyanotypes of Classical temples and prehistoric dwellings—created throughout Europe and the United States from the 1970s onward in parallel to her better-known work—to disclose the spiritual basis of her approach to light. Time grants us this vantage, but it also permits the opportunity to connect Kasten's work to her twenty-first century contemporaries. In Zeiger's essay, *Building, Rebuilding, Unbuilding*, the artist's

Crown Hall installation and *Architectural Sites* (1986–89) are discussed through the frame of architectural theory, while delving into how Kasten's work remains in conversation with new practitioners.

We remain indebted to the undertaking of *Stages*, devised by curator Alex Klein, which repositioned Kasten's history to unfasten the hold of photography's tether upon her work. In this release, both the multi-city exhibition and first comprehensive book brought (quite fittingly) transparency to decades of opacity surrounding the discussion of Kasten's pioneering contributions. Several unpublished series spanning past and present—from Kasten's *Amphora* (1995–96), *Dolmen* (1991–94), and *Temples* (1995–96), to her work created post-survey—compose this volume to approach her ongoing engagement with abstraction, light, and architectural form. The enduring fluidity of Kasten's practice, as evidenced here, is no more palpable than in her recent installations.

[1] "The Stages of Barbara Kasten," by Haley Weiss, *Interview Magazine*, 2015.
[2] Geoffrey Sonnabend, *Obliscence: Theories of Forgetting and the Problem of Matter* (Los Angeles: S.F.D.U.I. Press, 1991).
[3] Don DeLillo, *The Body Artist* (New York: Scribner, 2001), 94.
[4] Hans Ulrich Obrist, *Creative Chicago: An Interview Marathon*, September 29, 2018. Presented in partnership with the Chicago Humanities Festival and Art Design Chicago, a program of the Terra Foundation for American Art. Stage commissioned by Barbara Kasten, AON Grand Ballroom, Navy Pier, Chicago, IL.
[5] *The New Bauhaus*, directed by Alysa Nahmias, Opendox, 2019.

Artist/City (Crown Hall) (2018).
Installation view, S.R. Crown Hall,
Chicago, IL. Courtesy of the artist
and Bortolami, New York, NY

Crown Hall I (2018–19),
digital chromogenenic print.
54 × 40.5 inches (137.16 × 102.87 cm).
Courtesy of the artist, Bortolami,
New York, NY, and Corbett vs. Dempsey,
Chicago, IL

Crown Hall IV (2018–19),
digital chromogenenic print.
54 × 40.5 inches (137.16 × 102.87 cm).
Courtesy of the artist, Bortolami,
New York, NY, and Corbett vs. Dempsey,
Chicago, IL

Crown Hall II (2018–19),
digital chromogenenic print.
54 × 40.5 inches (137.16 × 102.87 cm).
Courtesy of the artist, Bortolami,
New York, NY, and Corbett vs. Dempsey,
Chicago, IL

Crown Hall V (2018–19),
digital chromogenenic print.
54 × 40.5 inches (137.16 × 102.87 cm).
Courtesy of the artist, Bortolami,
New York, NY, and Corbett vs. Dempsey,
Chicago, IL

Crown Hall III (2018–19),
digital chromogenenic print.
54 × 40.5 inches (137.16 × 102.87 cm).
Courtesy of the artist, Bortolami,
New York, NY, and Corbett vs. Dempsey,
Chicago, IL

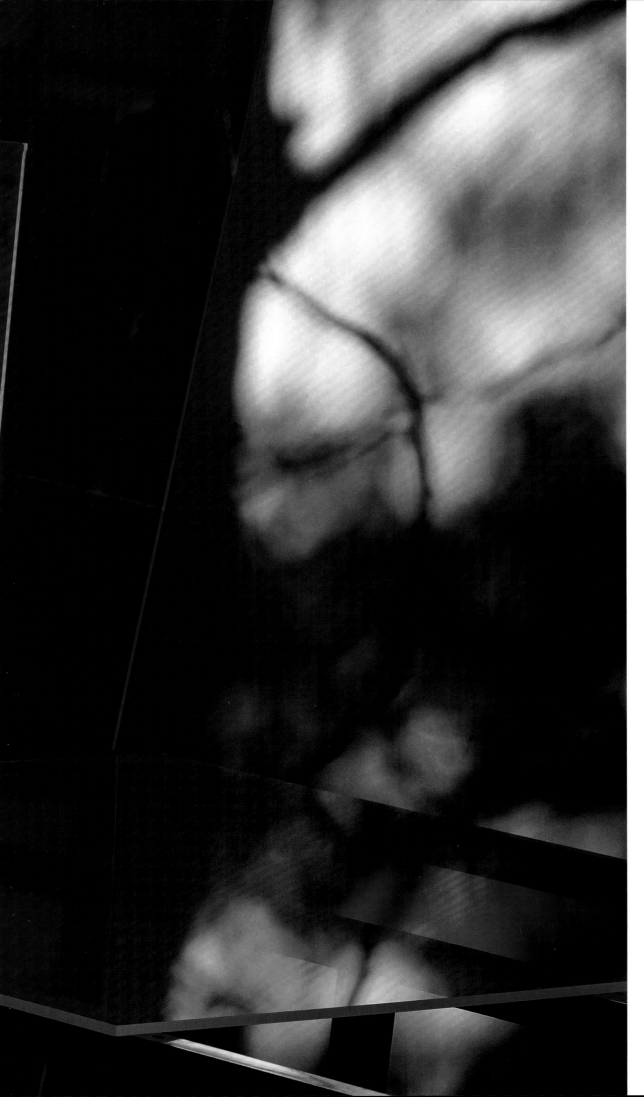

Crown Hall VI (2018–19),
digital chromogenenic print.
54 × 40.5 inches (137.16 × 102.87 cm).
Courtesy of the artist, Bortolami,
New York, NY, and Corbett vs. Dempsey,
Chicago, IL

Building, Rebuilding, Unbuilding

Mimi Zeiger

It never occurred to Barbara Kasten that she could be an architect. How could she, the daughter of a middle-class family growing up in Postwar Chicago, make buildings?

Her uncle was a draftsman—dragging graphite lines across thin sheets of paper; he knew blueprints, but not buildings. But just barely in her teens, Kasten, like most women of her generation, was burdened with the expectations of marriage and children—societal norms, both spoken and unspoken. Architecture was an unexplored imaginary. "I was always interested in the way things were put together and how they interacted," said Kasten one afternoon in her Chicago studio. There was some notion, some nascent dream of being an artist. "But that wasn't realistic either."[1]

What was realistic and what is now reality are two different things. As an artist, Kasten has spent her career defying the limitations set upon her. Her work fits uncomfortably within known categories: neither strictly photography, sculpture, performance, nor architecture. Operating within the overlaps and spaces in between, Kasten makes use of this liminal position as a tool for resistance—both in the name of abstraction and in the autonomy to exist as female artist. As such, Kasten's allegiances are found across a wide spectrum: from Bauhaus figures to contemporary practitioners using design and mixed reality to trouble similar questions.

Kasten often returns to buildings as ways to interrogate architectural space—to test boundaries and realities. Buildings, we are led to believe, are unequivocal objects: solid, hard, real. They matter. They are matter. This is even more apparent in Chicago, a city twice ravaged by fire in the late nineteenth century, reconstructed by Chicago Common Bricks—modular units of pink, red, and brown clay dredged up from the river—in place of flammable timber. Masonry is heavy: it carries its own weight as it struggles against gravity, the walls it builds are dense and impassable.

But then there is Crown Hall. Architect Ludwig Mies van der Rohe's steel and glass structure is everything that brick is not. It is, in his words "almost nothing."

The term "universal space" was one Mies often used to describe the seemingly weightless quality of this building and others, such as the Neue Nationalgalerie in Berlin, whose exterior steel frame allowed for a column-free, open-floor plan enclosed only by a glass façade. A mid-1950s photograph by Arthur Siegel pictures the architect standing behind his model for Crown Hall. It is the barest sketch of a building: a transparent rectangle graced by a formal stair that floats in the foreground. Mies, serious-faced and broad-shouldered, is commandingly posed with his arms outstretched, his unseen hands planted firmly upon table. In contrast, the scale model is a study in lightness. Through it, you can nearly see the buttons of his dark, double-breasted suit. Siegel's image conflates the model and the

man—one light, one heavy—into a single composition. The author is
inseparable from his creation.

Crown Hall opened in 1957 as the jewel of the Illinois Institute of
Technology (IIT) campus. Mies not only designed the master plan for the
campus but was also the head of the College of Architecture. Kasten, growing
up in Chicago's Bridgeport neighborhood, was a mere few miles west of IIT,
but the campus and its luminaries (including László Moholy-Nagy, then the
Director of the New Bauhaus) was still beyond her purview. By the time Crown
Hall was completed, she and her family had packed up and moved to Arizona.

Decades later, in the summer of 2018, Crown Hall became both the
subject and object of Kasten's project *Artist/City Crown Hall*. The installation
within the whole of the Miesian space commandeered the architecture
students' drafting tables and combined them into constructs alongside bright
planes of colored acrylic. The arrangements of steel frames—tilted, upended,
and balanced—took on glyphic characteristics.

Like much of her work, the pieces that composed *Crown Hall* existed as
neither solely photography nor sculpture, but rather simultaneously both. It
would be wrong to suggest that the drafting tables—bound with sheets of
fluorescent pink, orange, yellow, and blue—were props, and that the building
was simply an art directed backdrop. Installation and architecture are co-
dependent. In the experience of the installation and her images of the space,
also later exhibited alone, Kasten's constructs merge with Mies's structure to
form new geometries; they double as cast shadows, then triple as reflections
in the waxy surface of the building's black terrazzo floor. The architect's
tectonic perfection, so lauded for precision, is softened and rendered hazy.

Kasten has often credited the work and teachings of Moholy-Nagy
as an inspiration, specifically his photograms and cyanotypes—photographic
works made by directly placing objects on photosensitive medium without
the mediation of a lens. In his 1928 essay, "Photography is Manipulation
of Light" (written while at the Bauhaus Dessau, before his relocation to
Chicago), Moholy-Nagy argues against camera mechanics in favor of
immediacy and abstraction. He writes, "The light-sensitive layer—plate or
paper—is a tabula rasa, a blank page on which one may make notes with light,

just as the painter working on his canvas in a sovereign way uses his tool, brush, and pigment."[2] While Kasten worked with Crown Hall's ambient lighting—diffused sun that passes through frosted glass—and used a digital camera to make her images, within *Crown Hall* we can read Mies's building as a stand-in for that painterly canvas. The space receives the light and shadow cast across its surfaces made both of its own accord and by Kasten's additions. Attention to reflections and translucency, inherent to the site and the artist's work, only serves to heighten the abstraction.

It is important to note the fleeting temporality of the *Crown Hall* project. The installation stood in place for just six weeks, while students were away from the classes that continue there; in making the work, Kasten used readymade C-clamps and rubber-tipped spring clamps to secure the acrylic insertions to the steel tables and the building itself. The hardware remains visible in her photographs—there is no effort to disguise or erase these off-the-shelf tools. In fact, their very presence echoes Moholy-Nagy's photo-theoretical ambitions within the provisional and heuristic nature of the photograms, each image "an experimental gesture within the larger project of sensory and cognitive reform."[3] Site-specific interventions are often read as just that, an intervening—either a polemical upsetting or disruption—within a known space. This work, however, suggests a co-authoring, albeit temporary, shared between Kasten and Mies. "When most people see the photographs, they think that those are of the sculptures, but they are two different points of view,"[4] she explains.

"He is a master, you know," Kasten continues. "I don't know how he would feel about me being in his space. The goal was to get to know it more intimately way—to produce an exchange of ideas—like having conversation a between generations, between ways of thinking, between experiences."[5]

That designation "master" is not entirely reverential. For women who are artists, designers, and thinkers, especially of the second wave feminist generation, the gendered power construct that comprises the term "mastery" is complicated and cannot be quickly dismissed by chants of parity. It is a looming target, an ironic pause, or an exasperated sigh. And it denotes a singular kind of achievement relieved of any caveat of sex. To coauthor with a so-called master, then, is an act of rebuilding that requires both parties to find equal ground even when the canon grips tight to the status quo. "It is a power struggle to accept each other for our work,"[6] says Kasten.

Together with co-producer Deborah Irmas, in 1993 Kasten released the film *High Heels and Ground Glass*, which documented the lives of five women photographers whose contributions were at risk of being lost.[7] Among them were Gisèle Freund, whose lens captured postwar Berlin as a city in ruins before the wall, and Japanese photographer Eiko Yamazawa, who, like Kasten, experimented with color and abstraction.

Throughout Kasten's career, however, is an expression of feminism that is less interested in pat clichés of womanhood and artisthood—always hustling to escape the pigeonhole of "female artist" in the hopes of being evaluated independent of identity. Such a dance is always performed in the style of Ginger Rogers, backwards and in those proverbial high heels.

And yet that transcendence—of intersectional markers that bind authorship to gender, race, or sexuality—cannot be built on a past pitted by erasure. It requires rebuilding the historical narrative to correct for oversights and restoration of artistic agency.

"What I liked about the Bauhaus, especially the women, was the freedom that they enjoyed. Moholy-Nagy was not as involved with photography until his wife, Lucia Moholy, showed him how to make a photogram," says Kasten.[8] A photographer with a keen eye for portraiture, Moholy (née Schulz) was the author of some of the most famous images we know of the Bauhaus figures: a 1927 portrait of photographer Florence Henri (with whom Kasten corresponded as part of her research on *High Heels and Ground Glass*) is a frank document of a modern woman: cropped hair, arched penciled eyebrows, and an unflinching gaze.

Moholy married Moholy-Nagy in 1921, collaborating on the development of photograms and the philosophy/experimentation that would influence the Bauhaus workshops, before separating from him in 1929. As a Bauhaus documentarian, her photographs of the school in Weimar and the Bauhaus Dessau buildings designed by architect and founding director Walter Gropius are not only the default representations of things and structures, but they are also, according to Robin Schuldenfrei, "points of visual access to Bauhaus objects and to the ideas they were meant to instantiate."[9] To wit, the 1923 photograph of the director's office in Weimar illustrates via architecture, furniture, light fixtures, and textiles, the Modernist tenant of total integration of spatial practice with daily life. In 1933, Moholy fled Nazi Germany, leaving hundreds of her glass negatives behind. Gropius would later publish

and exhibit her photographs without attribution. For him, the credit-less images were evidence, proof of concept, and marketing tool for a shuttered Bauhaus. For Moholy, the photographs were witness to a place and time. Hers was a double absence: lost negatives and a lost authorship. The images circulated through museums and the media, which would take three decades and a lawyer to recover.

This narrative (an interlude, perhaps, within Kasten's) suggests the fraught equations between building and photograph, between architectural and artistic authorships, that are tinged with gender dynamics. Those aspects of the story, however, can be read in the context of Kasten's *Architectural Sites* series, developed in the mid-to-late 1980s, where architectural signature is complicated by photographic deviations.

The series began in 1986 with a commission from *Vanity Fair* magazine to photograph the entry lobbies of New York City's office buildings—a task meant to illustrate the Postmodern craze sweeping Manhattan architecture. Her photographs were never published—"I ended up being moved out by Leona Helmsley, or somebody like that, who had some kind of an affair—and that was the end of that," said Kasten in a 2018 lecture[10]—however, the experience of staging a piece outside the studio and within architectural space motivated her to continue the project independently. Throughout the rest of the decade, she photographed at multiple prestigious buildings across the United States—from Cesar Pelli's World Trade Center in New York to Bruce Goff's Pavilion for Japanese Art at the LACMA in Los Angeles. The resulting *Architectural Sites* developed into compositions of large-scale Cibachrome prints saturated with color and alive with vibrant geometries. In each, Kasten appropriates the signature architectural gestures of the structures and makes them her own. Colored gels, alongside the insertion of mirrors and other reflective surfaces, undermine the predictable spatial dynamics of the buildings.

Studies made in preparation for the *Architectural Site 17, August 29, 1988* (1988) shoot at the High Museum of Art in Atlanta, offer a glimpse into Kasten's meticulous working process. In her preparatory sketches, a Polaroid is marked with color temperatures in kelvins, later translated in situ by theater gels in vivid hues of cyan, yellow, and magenta. Richard Meier's architecture is formally dissected in a black and white photograph, bisected by a wedge of white paper. On site, the flimsy triangle is replaced by a large, knife-like mirror supported by a lighting stand. In the final image, the integrity of the museum's large atrium and sweeping catwalk is fragmented. The mirror reflects a muse-like statue cast in lurid night-club pink glow. What we call real turns toward the abstract—unspoken truths of perspective and gravity are compromised. Architecture as we know it is deconstructed, made uncanny. Kasten has unbuilt the building. Throughout the *Architectural Sites*, in place of the architecture of museums built for art, Kasten inserts the unseen performance of cinematic production. Her night shoots at the Whitney Museum of American Art or MOCA Los Angeles required full crews, as if on a film set; Kasten herself moving through the props and rigging like a director orchestrating each action.

Against these examples earlier in Kasten's career, *Crown Hall* finds particular resonance within the context of certain projects in contemporary architecture that negate tectonic logic. Mexican architect Frida Escobedo's installation *If we want to continue* (2017), presented on the ground floor of the Neutra VDL House as part of the exhibition *Tu casa es mi casa*, parallels the impulse to frustrate a clear understanding of the Modernist space.[11] Like Kasten, she plays with reflections to create abstracted and alternative architectures. For the piece, Escobedo inserted a mirrored wall diagonally between Seminar Room and the Music Room—the only oblique partition in a house built solely of right angles—to reflect the garden, transforming the space into a tropical panorama against the open curtains.

Architect Richard Neutra, of course, had his own interests in playing with transparencies and reflections. While Escobedo's installation recognizes his legacy, her gesture is bolder and more singular than Neutra's refined layering of real and reflected surfaces. There is a shared confidence with Kasten, whose *Architecture Sites* relied on a limited number of mirrored interventions—triangles, circles, spheres—to produce multi-spatial effects.

The collapse of many spaces into a single image, a hallmark of Kasten's practice, also presages more recent experiments in augmented reality (AR) and mixed reality (XR) undertaken by an emerging generation of architects and designers. In a 2018 installation, as part of their solo exhibition *Value in the Virtual* at The Swedish Centre for Architecture and Design (ArkDes) in Stockholm, Space Popular—a London-based design studio founded by Lara Lesmes and Fredrik Hellberg—negotiate between physical and virtual space. Thickly superimposed digital media collages occupy printed fabric scrims outstretched from ceiling to floor, held up by simple pipe scaffolding.[12] Their reliance on mundane, temporary materials to create a complex environment echoes Kasten's methods in *Crown Hall*. However, it is Lesmes and Hellberg's ongoing interrogation of what constitutes architecture, increasingly subject to new media conditions, which implies parallels with Kasten. For the catalogue that accompanies the exhibition, Space Popular put forth ten propositions for virtual architecture—a manifesto-like document that eschews reliance on real-world parameters for design. "The limitations that define our physical environment—such as gravity, light, or material resources—are of no concern in virtual worlds," write Lesmes and Hellberg. "As such, fundamental assumptions of what, how, why, and for whom architects design will be recast."[13]

Similarly, over the past few years, designer and media artist Leah Wulfman has drawn from effects in film sets and game production to create work that destabilizes understandings of what constitutes "real space" in an ever-immersive world. The 2019 film and installation *desert.vxf*, produced with Maxime Lefebvre, uses computer visioning and green screen paint slathered on oversized cutout shapes to blur the space between a desert landscape and the endless media found on the Internet

Like Kasten, Wulfman recognizes that the embodiment of the artist within their own staging is a vital act of artistic production They posit the term "gayming" as a descriptor for their practice, which brings together gaming technique and logics with queer identity. "Trans expression is inherently spatial and temporal," notes Wulfman in a 2020 interview. "The work is directly tied to a person occupying space, with their experiences, and there is the immediate need to play with and exist in space in order to even engage it."[14]

The "unbuilding" represented by the *Architectural Sites,* which carries through into Kasten's contemporary architectural interventions, constitutes a feminist act of resistance, a queering of the binary norms of the discipline. In his 2015 essay, "Use Your Illusion," historian Alex Kitnick draws parallels between Kasten's compositions and the site-specific cutting techniques used on abandoned buildings by artist Gordon Matta-Clark. Both present architecture as something to be dismantled—either physically or via illusion—by the camera lens.[15] Matta-Clark, trained as an architect before turning towards art, practiced *anarchitecture*. A portmanteau of anarchy and architecture, this approach operated in New York's downtown scene as a rebuttal to corporate architectural production and the lingering (and outmoded) Modernist ideologies of the 1970s. In 2018, scholar Jack Halberstam reevaluated Matta-Clark's particular strain of performative destruction in the essay "Unbuilding Gender." While history often aligns the artist with the earth or land art movements of the period, Halberstam rereads the work of Matta-Clark to suggest queer methodologies and vocabularies inclusive of trans and non-binary people. Namely, that the notion of a singular or idealized body/building must be destroyed, and that a multitude of possibilities exist within that destruction. As Halberstam writes, "Anarchitecture—almost by definition—cannot be embodied by an architect. It resists mastery, refuses to build, and finds other ways to alter the environments we move through, where we live and die."[16]

Kasten, working in New York and elsewhere just over a decade after Matta-Clark, illustrates an "other way"—a modality that defies the monographic celebration typical of architectural photography. Each of the structures she shot for *Architectural Sites* was by male architects, an unsurprising fact in a field where women even now make up less than twenty percent of registered practitioners. That this undoing is performed on film does not diminish the politic of the gesture since, within architecture, a representation of a space offers a near-equal proxy to the space itself. Indeed, artist and author Justin Beal argues that representation is the truer domain for architectural authority than a fully constructed building. As he writes, inserting the feminine pronoun as an *ex post facto* corrective, "A real architect is stuck working in the realm of representation. She does not make buildings; she

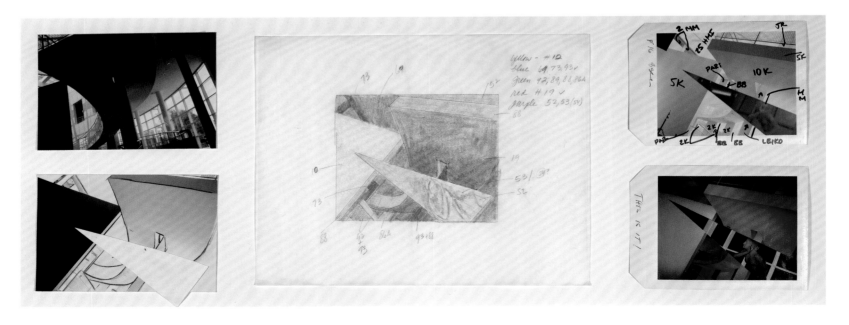

makes drawings and models and renderings and diagrams of buildings. She relinquishes control at the precise moment that idea becomes form."[17]

Kasten takes advantage of this inevitable surrender. Her work commences, even flourishes, as the architect—a Randian figure locked in the cultural imaginary—irrevocably cedes control. Unbuilding, then, cracks open architecture and allows abstraction to take over, and with it, possibilities for a radical rereading of the space, material, and form.

"There is a big political component to abstraction that Moholy-Nagy might have discovered when he was making photograms," notes Kasten. "It is not recognized enough for its ability to allow people to expect things that are not the norm."[18]

[1] Author interview with Barbara Kasten, Chicago, September 29, 2021.
[2] László Moholy-Nagy, "Photography is Manipulation of Light," *Bauhaus Photography* (Cambridge, MA: The MIT Press, 1985), 126, trans. Frederic Samson. Originally published in *Bauhaus, Zeitschrift für Gestaltung* vol. 2, no. 1 (Dessau: 1928).
[3] Michael W. Jennings, "László Moholy-Nagy Photograms," *Bauhaus 1919–1933: Workshops for Modernity* (New York: MoMA, 2009), 218.
[4] Author interview with Barbara Kasten, November 22, 2021.
[5] Author interview, November 2021.
[6] Ibid.
[7] Deborah Irmas and Barbara Kasten, *High Heels and Ground Glass* (New York: Filmmakers Library, 1993), 31 minutes.
[8] Author interview with Barbara Kasten, Chicago, September 29, 2021.
[9] Robin Schuldenfrei, "Images in Exile: Lucia Moholy's Bauhaus Negatives and the Construction of the Bauhaus Legacy," *History of Photography*, vol. 37, no. 2 (London: Taylor & Francis, 2013), 187.

[10] Barbara Kasten, "Connections: 48 Years," *MAS Context*, 2018 (accessed December 21, 2021).
[11] *Tu casa es mi casa*, Neutra VDL House and Studio, Los Angeles. Curated by Mario Ballesteros, Andrea Dietz, Sarah Lorenzen, and Mimi Zeiger. September 23, 2017–January 17, 2018.
[12] *Value in the Virtual: Space Popular*, ArkDes (Swedish Centre for Architecture and Design), Stockholm. Curated by James Taylor-Foster. September 19–November 18, 2018.
[13] Lara Lesmes and Fredrik Hellberg, "10 Propositions for Virtual Architecture," *Value in the Virtual*, 2018 (accessed January 17, 2022).
[14] Leah Wulfman, "Alum Leah Wulfman on 'Gayming' Architecture Beyond the Conceptual," SCI-Arc, 2020 (accessed January 17, 2022).
[15] Alex Kitnick, "Use Your Illusion," *Barbara Kasten: Stages* (Geneva: JRP | Ringier, 2015), 71.
[16] Jack Halberstam, "Unbuilding Gender," *Places Journal*, 2018 (accessed December 22, 2021).
[17] Justin Beal, *Sandfuture* (Cambridge, MA: The MIT Press, 2021), 57.
[18] Author interview, September 2021.

Hans Ulrich Obrist in Conversation with Barbara Kasten

Hans Ulrich Obrist: I wanted to begin at the beginning and ask you how you came to art, or how art came to you? Was there an epiphany?

Barbara Kasten: I went to Catholic school as a young girl. A nun, who was also an artist, did many of the murals for the church—paintings of the Blessed Virgin Mary, iconography of that nature. She took an interest in me. I must have shown talent; there was nothing to indicate that direction for me at home. We would go to the Art Institute of Chicago together to look at art.

HUO: Sometimes the future is invented with fragments of the past. Who were the artists that inspired you?

BK: Through out the years it changed. During the 1960s and '70s, when I was enrolled at the University of Arizona in Painting, it was the contemporary artists of the time I was most aware of, such as Mark Rothko and Helen Frankenthaler. When I moved to Los Angeles, I was particularly aware of artists like Robert Irwin, and we (my husband, [Leland Rice] I was married at the time) knew Jim Turrell as a student. I was informed about the Light and Space movement and thought what they were doing was interesting. It was during my time at the California College of Arts and Crafts in Oakland that I discovered the importance of the Bauhaus through Trude Guermonprez, who was a second-generation Bauhaus student. She had come to the United States from Germany to replace Annie Albers, who was on sabbatical at Black Mountain College. I was lucky enough to find her as a mentor.

HUO: So, for you, it was important I suppose also from the beginning that there was a connection between art and architecture.

BK: I am not exactly sure where the interest in architecture came from, but it was very strong. When I think back, it could have been just growing up in Chicago—I was very comfortable being downtown among the skyscrapers. By the time I lived in Europe in the 1960s, I was following architecture—not as a vocation but as an interest in structure, space, and monumentality.

HUO: How have architectural experiences impacted the evolution of your work? You were very inspired by your visit to Le Corbusier's Ronchamp Chapel, which is such a sculptural space. What did you learn from Ronchamp? How did it impact your approach to sculpture?

BK: Ronchamp gave me an experience of space that was absolutely unique. Being in its interior was the most important for me. I was not looking at it as an entity from the exterior, but instead through the atmospheric experience of

Intervention (2018). Installation view
with Barbara Kasten and Jeanne Gang,
*Creative Chicago: An Interview
Marathon* by Hans Ulrich Obrist,
Navy Pier, Chicago, IL. Presented
by the Chicago Humanities Festival
and Art Design Chicago supported
by the Terra Foundation for American
Art. Photo: David Kindler. Courtesy
of the artist

the inside—how light and color exchange to create an ambience that changes the very dimensionality of surfaces as sunlight falls and passes through the colored glass windows. How it conforms around, or rests on top of, surfaces inside. Ronchamp became an understanding and interpretation of what it meant to be *inside* a sculpture, instead of viewing a work as a complete object from the outside.

At the time, I was not yet interested in photography. Once I started working with the medium, that experience became central to how I thought about the light I was using on top of the elements I was putting together in the studio as either sculptural presentations or installations. I visited Ronchamp in 1965 and did not even start photographing until the 1980s. For twenty years it was with me.

HUO: Yes, and of course the architectural aspect is also present in your large-scale models, which we discussed as part of our *Creative Chicago: An Interview Marathon* in 2018. You built this amazing work for the stage, which has since been exhibited alone as a sculpture, but it also functioned as a speaking platform. All of this goes back to the 1970s, when you began building these large-scale models. I wanted to ask you to tell us a little bit about those, connecting to *Scenario* (2015), which was on view as part of *Barbara Kasten: Stages* (2015) at the Graham Foundation, during Chicago Architecture Biennial. What was the first one you built and how did they evolve?

BK: Well, I had initially began building these structures in a life-size scale so that I could be in the space and moving objects I had constructed—very simple geometric elements of sculpture. What brought them to life was the addition of light. I had used mirrors within these forms, so that when light hit their surface, it projected a kind of photogram on the walls. Once the light was turned off, the image vanished. This magical moment of lighting was an important concept around these forms. I found myself in the realm of photography because I was offered material from the Polaroid corporation—a kind of timely coincidence. I was not trained as a photographer, nor interested

Scenario (2015). Installation view, *Stages*, Graham Foundation, Chicago, IL. Photo: RCH | EKH. Courtesy of the artist

Le Corbusier, Ronchamp Chapel, Notre Dame du Haut, 1950–55. Ronchamp, France. © 2022 F.L.C. / ADAGP, Paris / Artists Rights Society (ARS), New York, NY

in a darkroom experience, yet the idea of having an instant recording material for these temporary environments was important. They were a kind of installation before installation was what it is today. Light was the key element, but it was the "photogram" aspect I carried from Ronchamp—that the projection of light falls within an atmosphere onto a surface that has its own contours, its own presence, and therefore changes its shape. That simple observation is what I took with me to these installations in the studio throughout the 1970s. Any ideas I have about photography came from the concept of the photogram, which as you know was László Moholy-Nagy's special roadway into abstraction. He talked about that in the film [*The New Bauhaus*, 2019] that you and I were both in—that the photogram was abstraction in itself. That has always been the trail: this light that I first experienced in architecture through Ronchamp.

HUO: We spoke about Moholy-Nagy while experiencing the amazing light of your piece, *Intervention* (2018), for the Marathon. It was pure magic. We also spoke about California, where you were living at the time—there was of course a lot of sunshine, but also a great deal of experimentation with industrial materials taking place during that era, such as in the work of Billy Al Bengston and Judy Chicago. Also, artists of the Light and Space movement, who were not only working with light but also combining the use of industrial materials. It was an incredible time in California, of experimentation, and your work kind of grew out of this experimental field.

BK: Right—it all came out of experimentation. I was very aware of the Light and Space artists, but we were experimenting differently with sources. Much of the illumination of their work was related to the environment and to the sunshine of California, whereas I relied more on the lighting techniques adopted by the movie industry—the theatricality and the simulation of a single light source. Even without being involved in Hollywood, seeing the materials they were using to transmit light was very interesting to me. Look at Robert Irwin, for example—his discs glowed. That was all an inspiration to me, but I took it indoors into a much more controllable environment. The installations were large-scale but possessed a regulated size; when you put a space like that into a photograph it becomes ambiguous. The image could be a document of anything from a miniature to the gigantic.

HUO: Your works have combined the photographic, the sculptural, and the painterly—in a way, one could say they are a Gesamtkunstwerk. What is your relationship to the notion of this concept? I think through the late Wagner the allusion came to mean something overwhelming, in a way, but I see your work as more of an "open Gesamtkunstwerk."

BK: Well, I think that "openness" has to do with my process. I was building, moving, and arranging these installations—yet from there, I would step out of the space and behind the camera. The photographs became a hybrid of my eye—what I took from being within the work and bringing it into the camera plane. Though, capturing space in two-dimensions has its own problems; I never wanted things to appear illusionistic, but both aspects were necessary to allow the viewer to come with me from one experience to another. I opened an avenue for perception and saw it as a performance that was not meant for an audience, though it could be translated as such.

Oskar Schlemmer, *Man and Art Figure* (ca. 1921). Courtesy of the VRI Slide Library of World Theater / Carl Richard Mueller. © Visual Resources, Inc.

Peter Fischli, David Weiss, *Natural Grace*, 1984, color photograph. 15 ³/₄ × 11 ⁷/₈ inches (40 × 30 cm). © Peter Fischli David Weiss, Zürich, Switzerland, 2022. Courtesy of Sprüth Magers, Berlin, Germany; Matthew Marks Gallery, New York, NY; and Galerie Eva Presenhuber, Zürich, Switzerland

Parallels I (2017). Installation view, *Parti Pris*, Bortolami, New York, NY. Courtesy of the artist and Bortolami, New York, NY

HUO: I want to come back to the sensitivity of architectural forms. We spoke about that during our Marathon interview in Chicago. You said that none of the works of sculpture you had done so far have elements that are attached to one another. They are all precariously balanced. That is also an interesting aspect of architecture: where cantilevers look as if they are ready to fall but are balanced by the rest of the structure. I love this idea of the equilibrium—it goes back to an early encounter I had with Fischli/Weiss's film of a chain reaction, *The Way Things Go* (1987). Before that, their *Equilibres* (1984–86) pictured objects on the cusp of collapsing. I am really interested in this idea that none of your works have elements that are permanently attached. Can you talk about this in relation to architecture, specifically this idea of cantilevers, which look as if they are ready to fall?

BK: Exactly—the decision to exclusively construct from leaning forms, which will only stand in a particular way, is significant. That is ultimately what designates the shape; it is not a translation of a drawing, which is the approach most architects would have, but more about what the material is telling me it wants to do. That is why I think many of the forms I use in building these sets rely on basic shapes. In *Parallels I* (2017), I kept pushing the stack of several flourescent acrylic beams as far out as I could get them to go without collapsing. That was the magic moment: when the form managed to just stay there. You know that there is a sense of precariousness, but also a sense of beauty as the work checks itself. You cannot do that in conventional architecture, but it can be done when you are working with the forms that come from architecture.

HUO: Are there any living architects you wish to collaborate with?

BK: The closest I came are in the photographs *Architectural Sites* (1986–89).

HUO: Right—that is another relationship to architecture in your work, where you staged photographs using mirrors in these in these Postmodern buildings.

BK: It was all an experiment—to take an existing piece of architecture and use it as an element in my photographs. The process was the same building a set in my studio, except that some of the aspects of space were in place already. I wanted my work to not just complement the situation, but through the

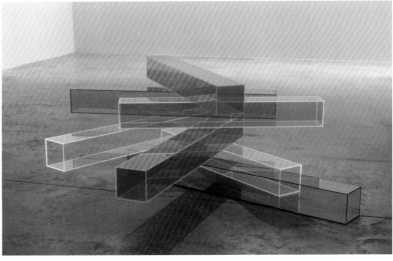

insertion of mirrors and forms to also analyze and dissect. To see the building from other points of view. The *Architectural Sites* presented a collaboration with something that was already complete. I spoke with most of the architects; Arata Isozaki was the most pleased. I met him in Japan and he opened his arms to the fact that somebody was taking his work and doing something beyond what he had done. The series as a whole was not well-accepted at the time—critics saw the idea of injecting myself into that kind of space as somehow questionable—and it took twenty years before people saw those works in a new perspective. This generation is much more open to what photography can be, artists are freer to mix mediums now than they were in the 1980s. There is a fluidity of practice in my work that is now matched. At the time, there was this immense pressure to "decide" between the art world, the architecture world, or in the design world. I never really wanted to decide.

HUO: Your work anticipated so much of this fluidity of practice we see now. We touched upon it briefly, but of course Mies van der Rohe is important in relation to the installation you did at Crown Hall, but also the iterations of that work for both Chicago Marathon piece and in the Paramount Studios installation you did for Frieze LA. Could we hear more of your reflections on Mies's work and the importance of it?

BK: You know, I grew up in Chicago from 1936–55 not far from Crown Hall, but by the time it was built in 1957, I had already moved with my family to Arizona. Returning to Chicago decades later and realizing that Mies's work was sort of

in my backyard it became an obvious place to consider hosting an installation [*Artist/City (Crown Hall)*, 2018]. I had long felt the importance of the building—the composition, the innovative ceiling structure—standing inside the grand hall of the space itself was akin to standing inside Ronchamp. Both are dependent on the light that emanates from the space itself. Crown Hall presented a unique challenge for me, given the emphasis on natural light, whereas I was used to incorporating theatrical lighting. And yet, I wanted to present another perspective of that space—using the atmosphere but denying the light that Mies had designed. Photographing the installation was merely another way of expanding my own vocabulary.

HUO: Our Marathon took place on a stage designed by you with pieces from *Crown Hall*.[1] The Grand Ballroom at Navy Pier was a very different building. You said that in *Intervention* you wanted to honor Mies and Moholy-Nagy, these two great immigrants to Chicago, and of course the link to the Bauhaus. How did you see the connection between these works—from the Modernist glass box to its place within an ornate structure?

BK: Right—it is a whole different experience, from the Beaux-Arts ballroom to the Modernist structure of Mies, which could be considered a clash of styles or forms. That is always the challenge: to integrate parts of life that do not look like they fit together, which is part of the whole immigrant experience. The process of making art is probably the most important aspect that connects the concept of *Intervention*. The work did not start out with a sketch, design, or completed form—but instead developed as one element was added to another.

I think that is what makes art live, allowing experience into the act of creation that the audience somewhat completes. Location inherently adds a different element to a work's history and completeness. That same work was shown at Frieze Los Angeles the following year (*Intervention*, 2019), where it was installed inside of a movie set scenery within Paramount Studios. It was

Norman Foster, Hong Kong and Shanghai Bank Headquarters, 1979–86. Photo: Nigel Young. © Foster + Partners

James Stirling, Neue Staatsgalerie, 1979–84. © Staatsgalerie Stuttgart, Stuttgart, Germany

like taking it back to the innards of the structure—a stage—that I had begun working with decades prior.

HUO: When we talk about Mies, you were not only inspired by Crown Hall, but also in the 1970s by Neue Nationalgalerie in Berlin.

BK: Yes, I saw the Neue Nationalgalerie at the beginning of my quest to find out what I wanted to do with my life. I think I returned to the potential transparency of a building when I started making some works in the studio in 2010–11. I was working with clear Plexiglas and wanted the subject matter to have no equivalency to a form that could be identified; it had to be something for the material itself. In that glass transparency of the Neue Nationalgalerie, Mies got it—he gave me the shadows, which I needed. Light is shadow. Everybody speaks of light, but you can only see light when it creates a shadow to identify itself.

HUO: Right, all these encounters add up and stay as another architectural experience. Following that, you visited the Norman Foster bank building in Hong Kong, completed in the 1980s. What was it about the Foster building that inspired you?

BK: I was going to Japan and wanted to be able to see it while I was nearby. The building had been described to me by a curator in New York as a structure in multiple layers with an enormous escalator that dissected the center of the building—another instance of transparency. All of that was very intriguing to me and was not something I wanted to see in a photograph, but rather in person. I made my way there to make sure I could live within and walk through it. I visited some buildings in Stuttgart after that trip, as well.

HUO: The Weissenhof-Siedlung Estate, model houses for a different society for different living? Just outside the city, built in 1927.

BK: Yes—that and the James Stirling Neue Staatsgalerie Stuttgart. At the time, I was just starting to learn more about architecture and what was happening. The motivation was to go and experience these iconic buildings—a kind of pilgrimage. I also went to see the models and costumes of the famous Bauhaus Experimental Theater led by [Lothar] Schreyer and [Oskar] Schlemmer. That ended up influencing the costumes I did with the Margaret Jenkins Dance Company during a residency at Capp Street Project in San Francisco in 1985.

HUO: In your work there is also the obvious connection to theater—can you speak about the importance of stages in your work?

BK: I had realized that the stages I built in the studio to photograph *Construct* in the 1970s could be used in many ways. I was always part of the performance within the stage while I was making the photographs. Approaching the collaboration in San Francisco, it seemed natural to adopt that logic. I made some parts of the set movable to echo how I would move the forms within the installation I was photographing. In this way, the dancers became me.
All of this relates to the Bauhaus: how the process of things comes through the artist and evolves into whatever is at hand. I saw the stage as an enlargement of my studio. That was how the videos came along—movement was an element that was previously missing in the tableaux (the only movement at present was my own while photographing).
I choreographed the films, not just as found glimpses of life but as the movement of light through form. It was all so interconnected.

HUO: One thing I was also wondering is that you say that the Internet and digital technologies are providing fertile ground for artists today. It has made photography a broader category, though that remains an open question, but has also led to an expanded notion of photography. I was curious how Tim Berners-Lee's invention—the World Wide Web in 1989—either changed, or augmented, the way you work?

BK: I had to find a way to continue working throughout the first year of pandemic isolation—in preparation for my solo exhibition at the Aspen Art Museum [*Scenarios*, 2020–21] I used digital processes in a way that I likely would have never done were it not brought on by the lockdown. Did you know that I was part of a program that Adobe and Apple sponsored in the early 1990s, when the computer was first being introduced to artists? They did a program in Maine that invited artists across different disciplines to be taught the basic techniques of Photoshop when the application was still in the process of being developed. Then, as now, technology has never really interested me in terms of imagery, but rather in my ability to do something else. During that residency I learned techniques that I used later to make a 40-foot-long diorama that was digitally printed on canvas, based on a collage of four by five images I photographed in Terragona, Spain, as part of a satellite commission for the Barcelona Olympics [*El Medol*, 1992]. The machine served me in way of creating a composite, but not in terms of creating the image.

Elevation (2020). Installation view, *Scenarios*, Aspen Art Museum, Aspen, CO. Photo: Simon Klein. Courtesy of the artist

HUO: And of course, you use technology with your videos to augment perception. I remember when I saw your exhibition at the Graham Foundation in 2015, specifically the work *Scenario*, where you projected video onto a structure that you built from geometric shapes that were similar to the shapes in the projected image.

BK: I am not an "intellectual artist." I really work from an experiential point of view. This augmented reality concept was not something I was thinking about in those terms. Instead, I thought how interesting it would be to have smaller forms projected upon at a larger scale; to optically expand the stage set. It was really an experimental idea of taking what I know about photography, and movement, and blowing it up. The work made you wonder how all these forms were moving, and how they were generated. A changing scenario of light and form. That was all achieved through the merging of two different processes: one of building the set, and the other of filming that same set. Some of the built forms I used were repurposed from other installations. A lot of what I save in the studio acts as kind of as resource material for future work and comes from a question: how could I make this in a way that presents a challenge of reality to the viewer?

HUO: Have you made any new video pieces over the last couple of years?

BK: I am working on some now since *Scenarios*. I had created several new works for Aspen in a conceptual manner based on what I knew would likely happen in certain light and certain conditions. One work was a mirrored form against the entrance wall of the exhibition that reflected the woven façade by Shigeru Ban [*Elevation*, 2020]. It was a sculpture, but I like to think of it as a video; it traced the daylight changing within the building as it passed through the grid of the building onto the reflective surface of the work. Nature added the movement, but I captured it and used it as you would a film. The grid became his and mine, without us really "collaborating" in the conventional sense.

HUO: Also, your "collaboration" with sacred sites. For example, you have been very inspired by the Puye Cliff Dwellings, which are ruins of an abandoned Pueblo in the Santa Clara Canyon.

BK: Yes—I visited the cliff dwellings, a prehistoric religious site made of soft volcanic material, in the 1990s. In a couple of the photographs I took, there was a partially round building, a Kiva, used on the ceremonial ground. The environment itself, the ruins, were built into the cliffs as living environments. I sought out the site as a kind of a spiritual thing—I also did some investigations and photographs of dolmen, these Neolithic stone monuments, in Brittany around the same time. My father had just passed away; the choice of using the architecture as a symbol for this loss was very personal.

HUO: And many were goddess sites, which you have visited and revisited over the years. It would be interesting to hear more about how you have approached the sacred through a feminist lens.

BK: Well, that is an interesting question. I always felt the Dolmens were a very feminist kind of architecture because of the structure itself, their tunnels and entrances into wider kind of womb-shaped room, as an indication of holding power. That was my initial attraction to it. In *Mané Rutual* (1994), I made a

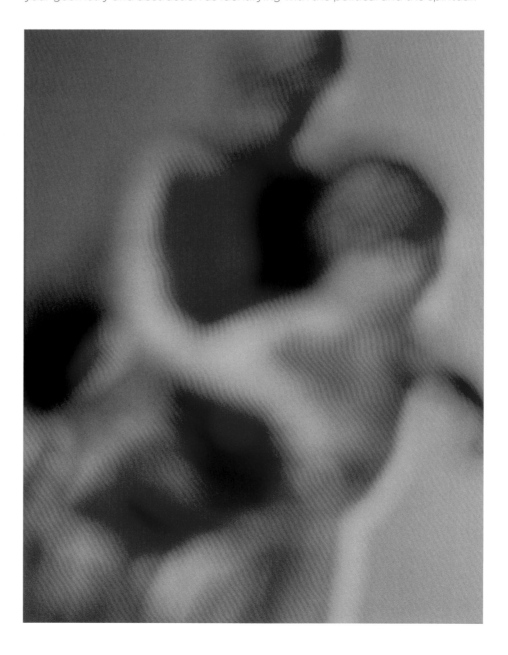

Tanagra Goddess I (1995), cibachrome.
5 × 4 inches (12.7 × 10.16 cm).
Courtesy of the artist

composite of three different smaller Dolmens to appear as a continuous site. I also captured images of goddesses that were placed in women's burial chambers in Greece around 300 BCE [*Tanagra Goddess*, 1995], as well as other locations. Around this time, I was doing a residency at Cornell University, where I discovered various funerary figures of women in quotational quotidian gestures. Some were reminiscent of the person who it was buried with embedded in the objects. I began looking for other structures, other important indicators, of an afterlife. The inherent feminism of the structures was a discovery I made along the way. When I found the Dolmens, which are thousands of years old, I had to honor evidence of an ancient history that portrayed women in power.

HUO: I wanted to touch upon another dimension of abstraction now in your current work. When we were in Chicago, during the marathon interview I told you about César Domela, whom I befriended as a student—he was in his nineties when I met him—and was an old friend of Piet Mondrian in the 1930s. He told me that Mondrian had no tolerance for things that were not at a right angle. You also are a perfectionist, and geometry plays a very big role in your work. Do you see your geometry and abstraction as identifying with the political and the spiritual?

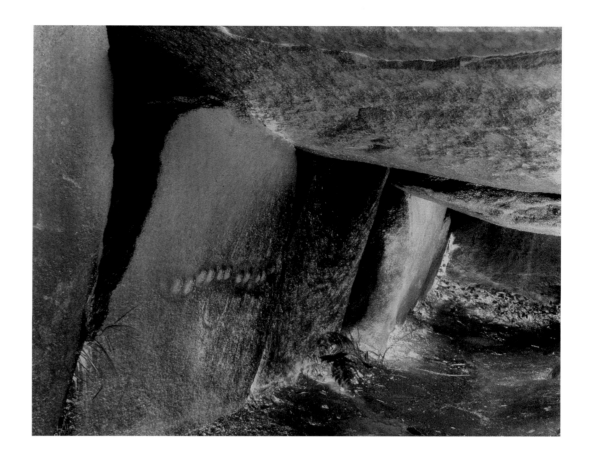

BK: I think in looking at my photographs in the beginning, people have identified design, color, and form—but have not taken their references further into the meaning or reasons behind why these forms are set up the way they are. I see them as an encouragement to look and see through a new perspective. In concept, this might prepare one to do the same in life, politically or otherwise. So, in this very simple and direct way, my work has a very active political possibility. That was the perspective that the Bauhaus took as well—design for the masses, which would create another kind of political movement. I want to remind people to think differently through abstraction; it is what one gets out of looking at a form, but also has a history in motivating openness to change. I think that needs to be examined more by people who have ways of expressing verbally—the only thing I can do is to continue to make experiences that are not visible until I make them visible. And that involves having some power behind it.

HUO: Returning to your sculptures, it is relatively little known that you used to work with textiles.

BK: Well, many of them do not exist anymore. There were three of the textile sculptures [Seated Forms, 1972] in the Stages exhibition at the ICA Philadelphia, the Graham Foundation in Chicago, and at the MOCA Pacific Design Center in Los Angeles. They are few of the surviving ones from the series I made while when I was on a Fulbright in Poland. They derived from a tapestry concept that was used in the Bauhaus, which is what Guermonprez, my mentor, experienced as a student—or the way that Magdalena Abakanowicz created her dimensional forms, which were all made as flat tapestries. I also relied on my own experiences as a young woman, making clothes for myself, many of the techniques of creating form from a flat piece of

Dolmen (Kerguntuil) (1991), digital archival pigment print. 20 × 24 inches (50.8 × 60.96 cm). Courtesy of the artist

fabric I incorporated into the weaving. I created darts—pulling together the weft and the warp—so I could create volume. I used that process in trying to shape something flat into something three dimensional. From those forms came the *Figure/Chair* works (1973), which featured diagrammatic images of a young nude female student in a chair using the same material used to draw blueprints. Starting with those textiles, my interests in theatricality, installation, and presentation in the round were evident—I was not interested in showing just a flat work on the wall.

HUO: That is beautiful. What role would you say that chance plays in your work?

BK: It certainly presents itself, but it is a matter of how much I take it and use it. There is a lot of chance in how I find materials, sometimes from invitations to do certain projects that I might not have dreamed up for myself. Or when somebody sees something unusual and thinks of me and what I might be able to do with it. I really love that aspect of it.

HUO: My recurring question has to do with the unrealized project, which manifests itself in many ways. Perhaps public art commission entries, which often happen through competitions. Or dreams, utopias, that are either too big or too expensive to be realized. Censorship can be a reason why a project is not realized—as my friend Doris Lessing often points out, there are of course certain projects one *wants* to do but does not *dare* to do, which is a form of self-censorship. Do you have any unrealized projects, unbuilt roads, you could mention?

Seated Form (green) (1972),
handwoven sisal and Thonet chair.
Approximately 35 × 25 × 25 inches
(88.9 × 63.5 × 63.5 cm).
Photo: Thomas A. Nowak.
Courtesy of the artist

Seated Form (red) (1972),
handwoven sisal and Thonet chair.
Approximately 35 × 25 × 25 inches
(88.9 × 63.5 × 63.5 cm).
Photo: Thomas A. Nowak.
Courtesy of the artist

BK: I do not have a specific project, but I think it would be to occupy a position where I could do something greater than the scope of anything I have done so far. I want to create a team of people to help me realize something that is bigger than myself, or than I can do on my own. What remains unrealized is something monumental—not necessarily in scale, but in complexity. I need a challenge, and I am waiting to see if somebody comes up with a great one for me. It would be great if I could have that chance to prove something beyond what most people think I do.

October 31, 2021

Figure/Chair (1973),
diazotype on newsprint.
22 × 17 inches (55.88 × 43.18 cm).
Photo: Thomas A. Nowak.
Courtesy of the artist

¹ *Creative Chicago: An Interview Marathon*,
September 29, 2018. AON Grand Ballroom,
Navy Pier, Chicago, IL.

Works 2015–2020

Crossover (2020). fluorescent acrylic, paper, HD video (color, silent, 5:51 minutes). Dimensions variable. Installation view, *Scenarios*, Aspen Art Museum, Aspen, CO. Photo: Carter Seddon. Courtesy of the artist

Scenarios (2020). Installation view, Aspen Art Museum, Aspen, CO. Photo: Carter Seddon. Courtesy of the artist

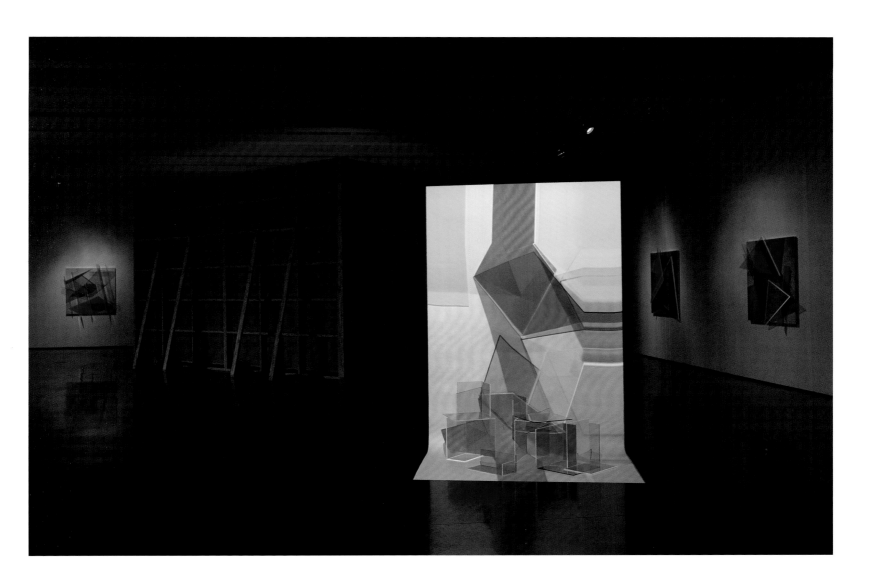

Elevation (2020), mirrored acrylic.
105 × 208 ½ × 5 ⅛ inches
(266.7 × 529.6 × 13 cm).
Installation view, *Scenarios*,
Aspen Art Museum, Aspen, CO.
Photo: Simon Klein.
Courtesy of the artist

Scenario (2020), wood, plaster,
HD video (silent, color, 3:38 minutes).
9 × 12 × 18 feet (2.74 × 3.65 × 5.48 m).
Installation view, *Scenarios*, Aspen Art
Museum, Aspen, CO. Photo: Carter
Seddon. Courtesy of the artist

Scenario (2020), wood, plaster, HD video (silent, color, 3:38 minutes). 9 × 12 × 18 feet (2.74 × 3.65 × 5.48 m). Installation view, *Scenarios*, Aspen Art Museum, Aspen, CO. Photo: Carter Seddon. Courtesy of the artist

Following pages
Sideways (2015/2020), HD video (silent, color, 3:30 minutes). Dimensions variable. Installation view, *Scenarios*, Aspen Art Museum, Aspen, CO. Photo: Carter Seddon. Courtesy of the artist

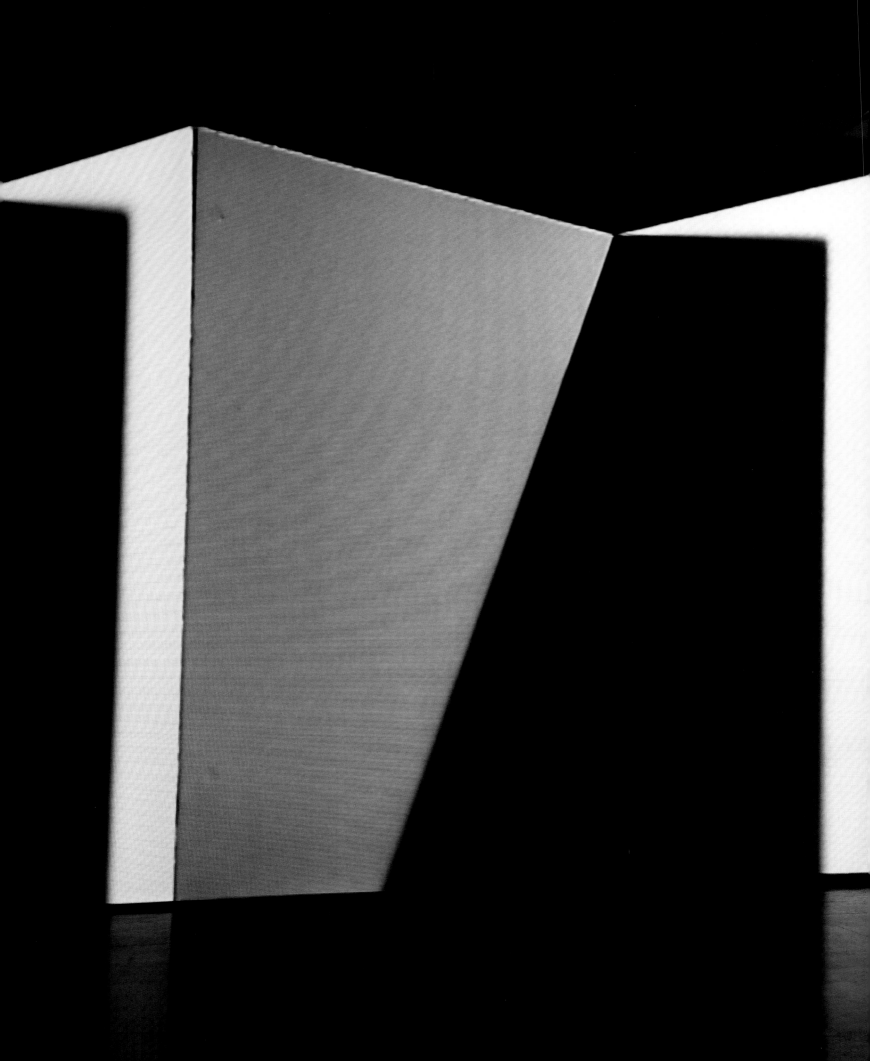

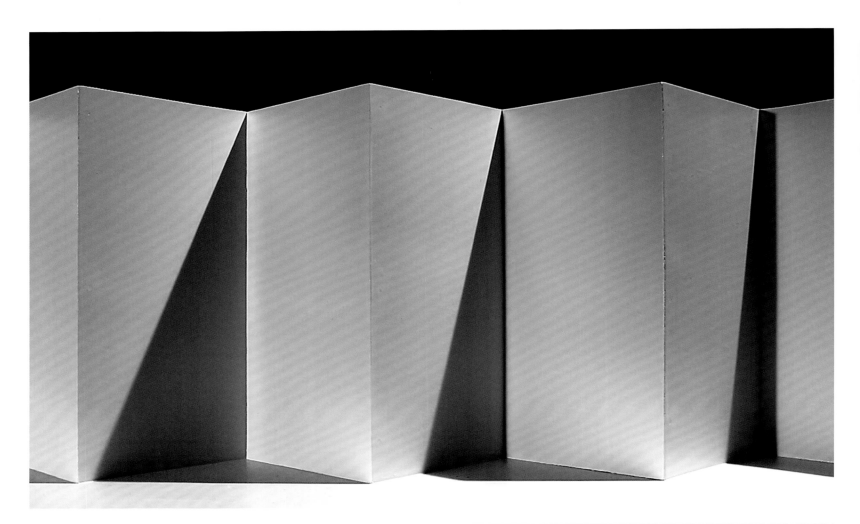

Stills from *Sideways* (2015/2020).
Courtesy of the artist

Following pages
Parallels (2017), fluorescent acrylic.
32 × 98 × 96 inches (81.5 × 249 × 244 cm).
Installation view, *Scenarios*, Aspen Art
Museum, Aspen, CO. Photo: Carter
Seddon. Courtesy of the artist

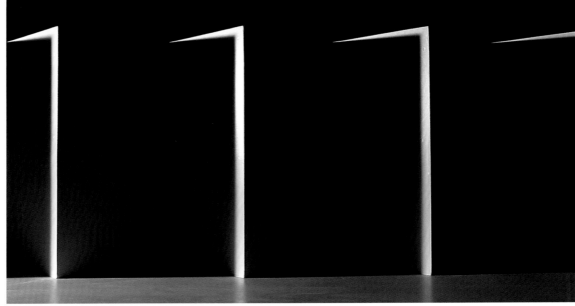

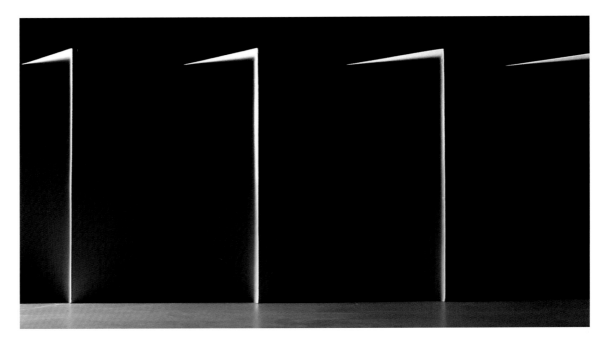

Collision 121 (2019),
digital chromogenic print.
48 × 84 inches (121.92 × 213.36 cm).
Courtesy of the artist and Kadel
Willborn Gallery, Düsseldorf, Germany

Collision 122 (2019),
digital chromogenic print.
48 × 84 inches (121.92 × 213.36 cm).
Courtesy of the artist and Kadel
Willborn Gallery, Düsseldorf, Germany

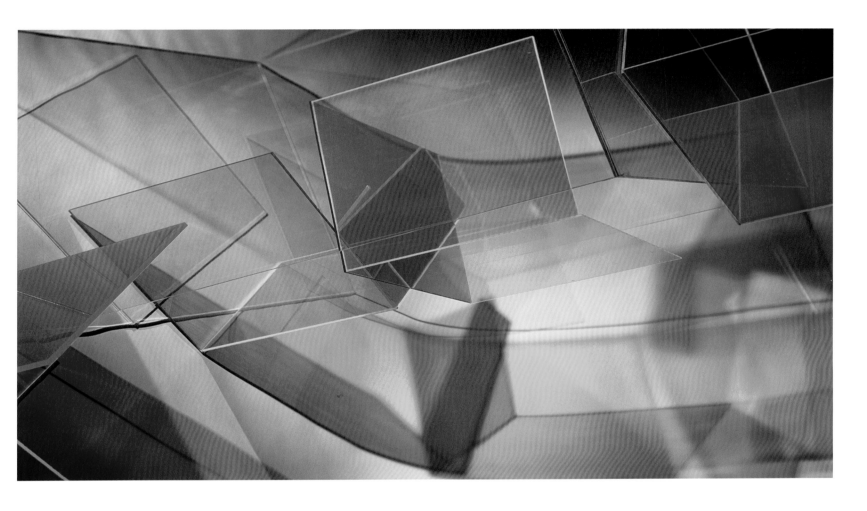

Parallels I (2017), fluorescent acrylic. 32 x 98 x 96 inches (81.5 x 249 x 244 cm). Installation view, Bortolami, New York, NY. Courtesy of the artist and Bortolami, New York, NY

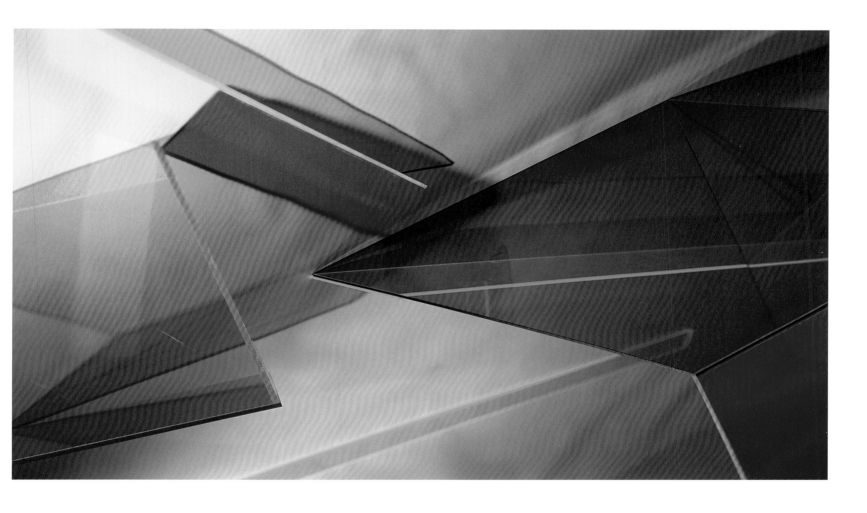

Revolutions (2017), paper, HD video (silent, color, 3:47 minutes). Dimensions variable. Courtesy of the artist and Thomas Dane Gallery, London, UK

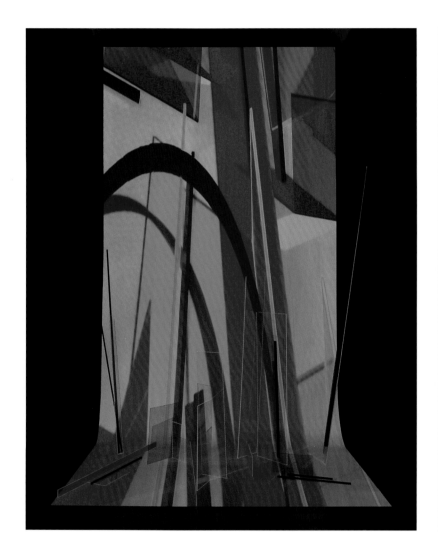
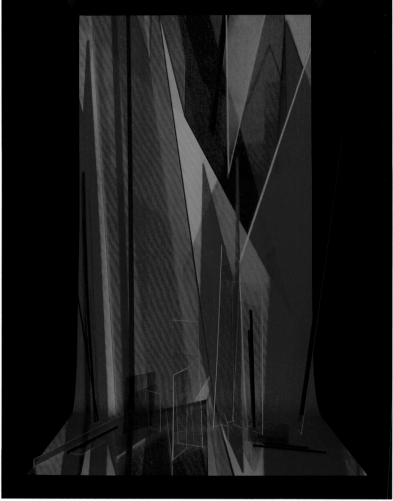

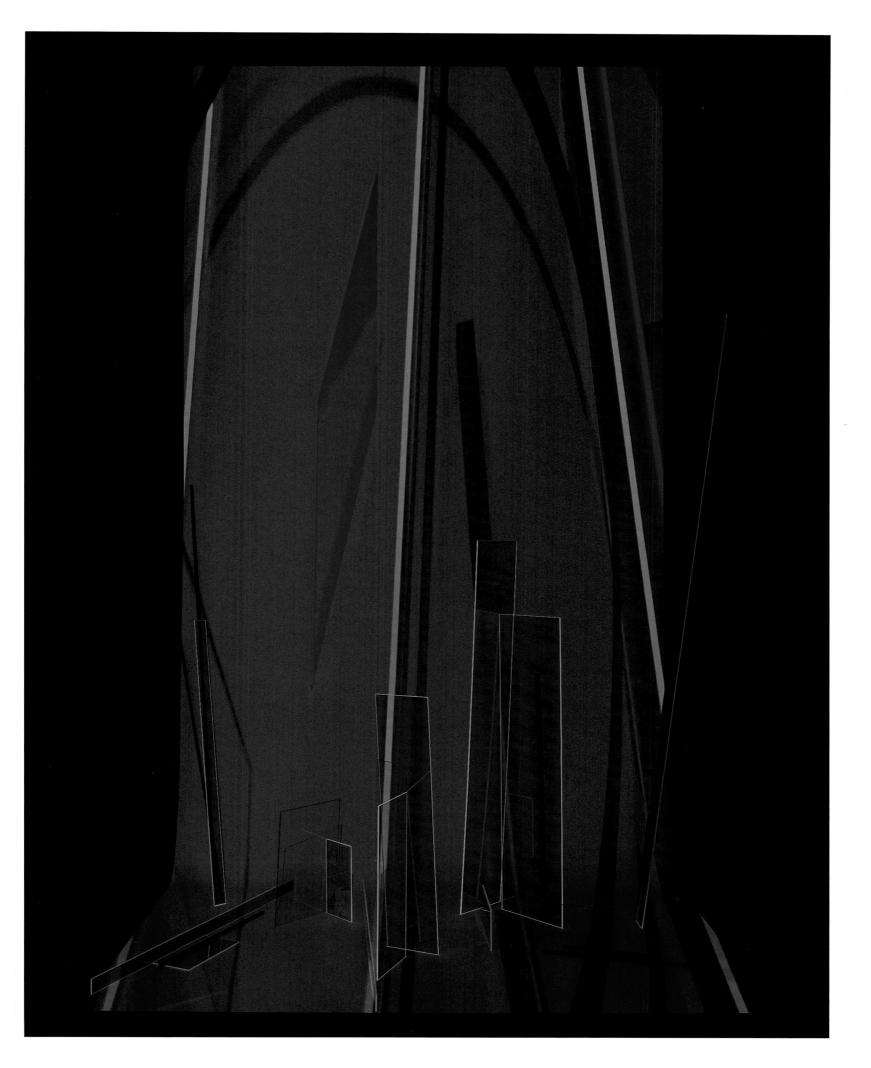

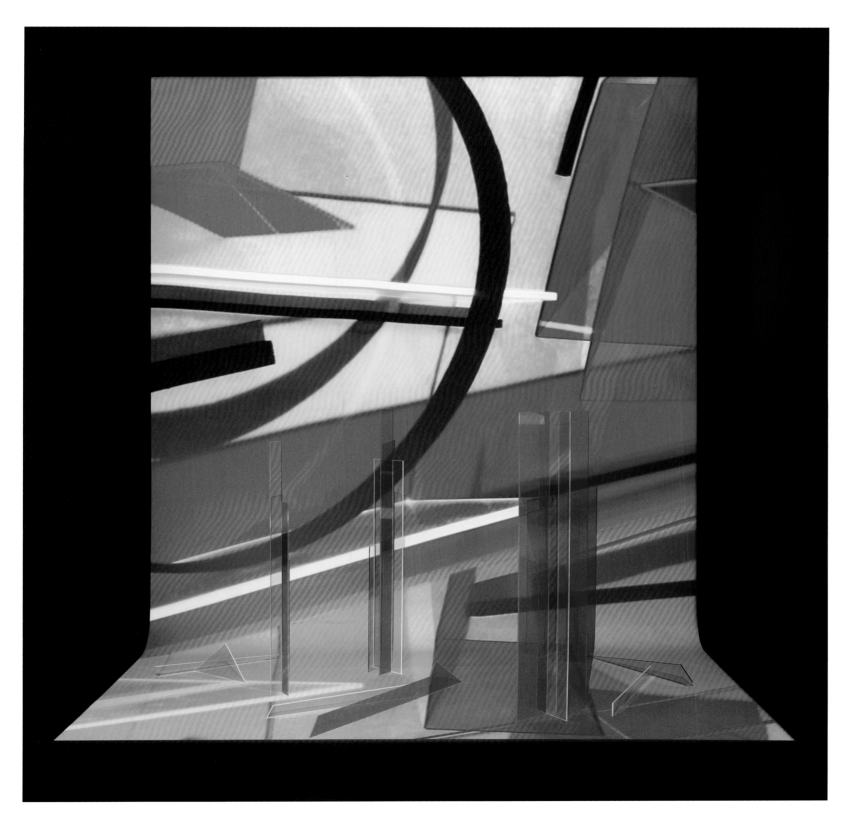

Axis (2015), HD video (silent, color, 5:20 minutes). Dimensions variable. Photo: Constance Mensh. Courtesy of the artist and Institute of Contemporary Art, University of Pennsylvania, Philadelphia, PA

Sideways Corner (2016), HD video (silent, color, 8:19 minutes). Dimensions variable. Courtesy of the artist and Kadel Willborn Gallery, Düsseldorf, Germany

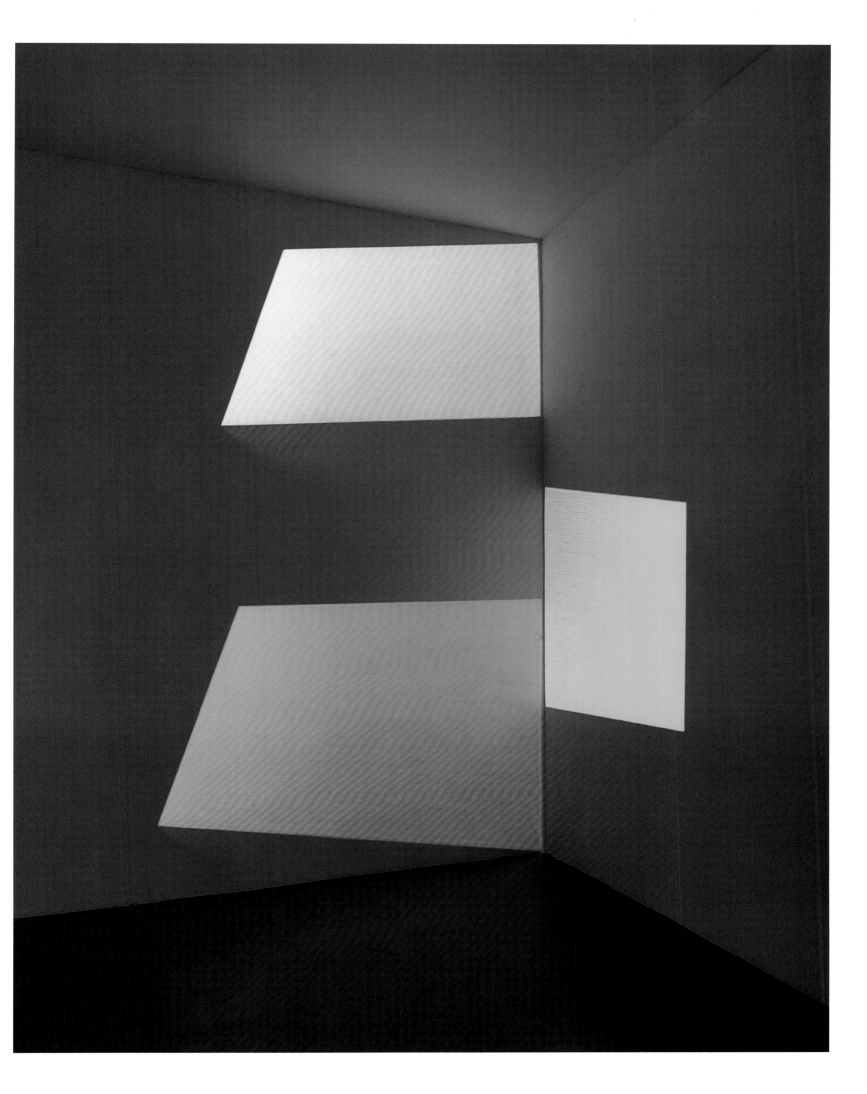

Futurism (2020). Commissioned by the City of Toronto, Private Developer Percent for Public Art Program, Toronto, ON. Courtesy of the artist

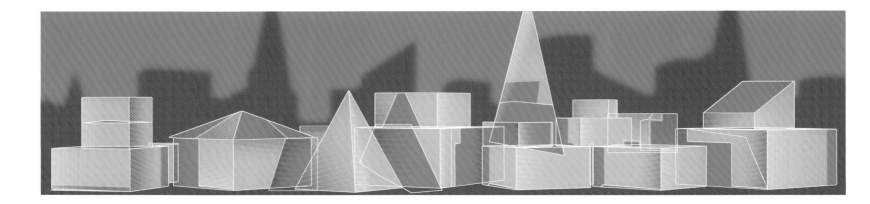

Sideways Corner (2016), HD video (silent, color, 8:19 minutes). Dimensions variable. Courtesy of the artist and Soluna Festival, Dallas, TX

Inside Out (2020), fluorescent acrylic, steel. Installation view, *Works*, Kunstmuseum Wolfsburg, Wolfsburg, Germany. Photo: Andreas Beitin. Courtesy of the artist

Sideways Corner (2016), HD video (silent, color, 8:19 minutes). Dimensions variable. Installation view, *Stages*, MOCA Pacific Design Center, Los Angeles, CA. Courtesy of the artist

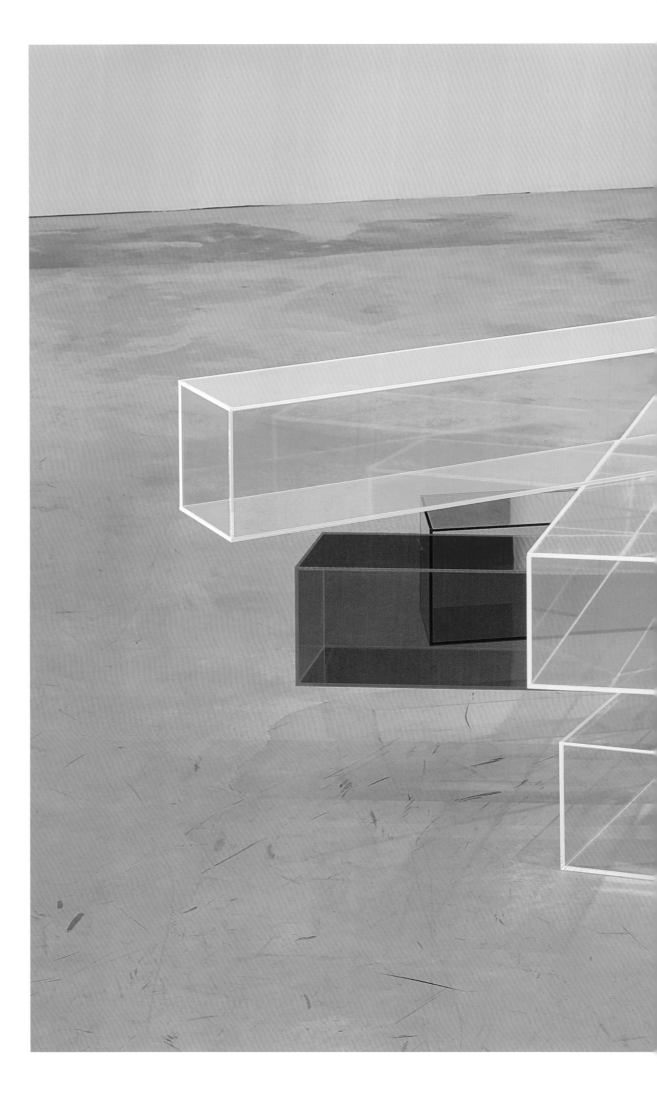

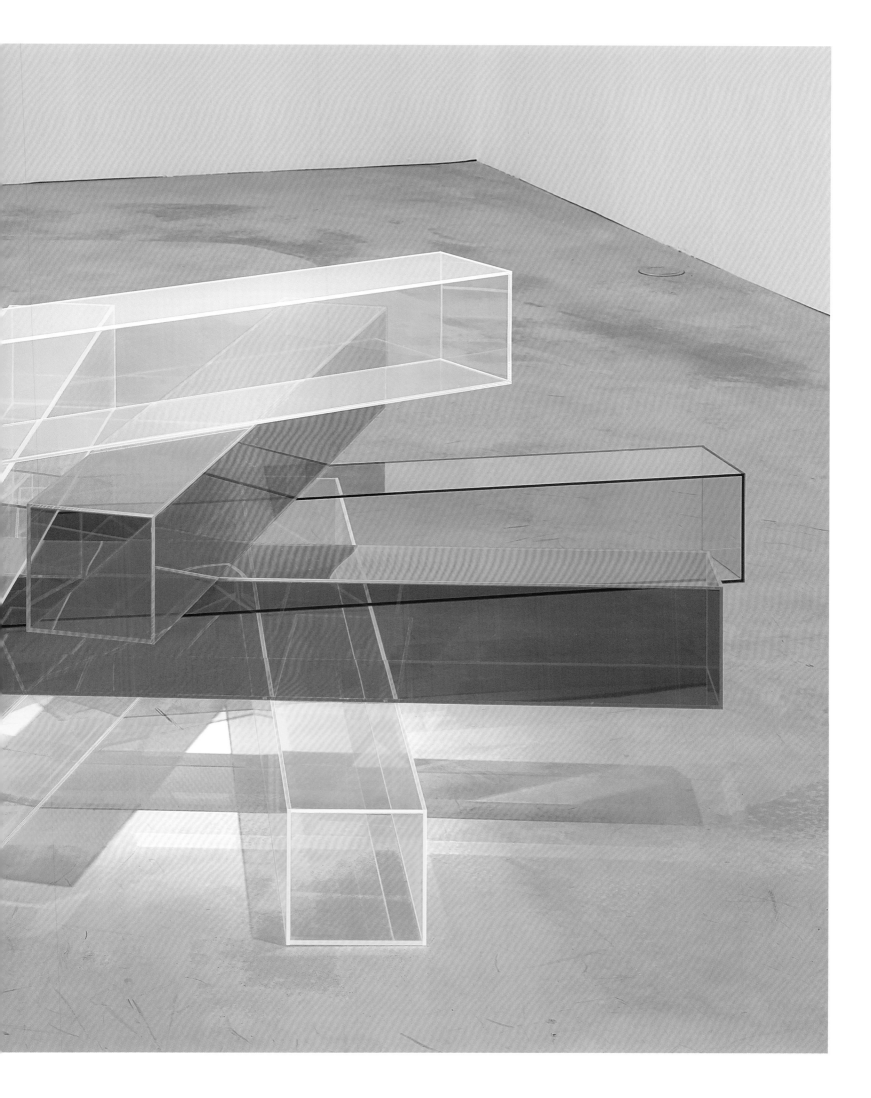

Scenario (2015), wood, plaster, HD video
(silent, color, 3:38 minutes).
9 × 12 × 18 feet (2.74 × 3.65 × 5.48 m).
Installation view, *Stages*, Graham
Foundation, Chicago, IL.
Photo: RCH | EKH. Courtesy of the artist

On Goddesses and Sacred Sites:
Scenes for Barbara Kasten

Stephanie Cristello

Dancers clothed in white occupy the stage. Silhouettes of pyramids and Corinthian columns frame an artificial landscape of light where their bodies perform contractions, extensions, and arabesques. Fragments of mirrors—at times like a pool of water or sharp like jagged glass—record their movement in cascading reflections, shadows cast in jewel-toned hues that wrap around the construction in gradations of ruby, sapphire, and gold. The scene appears like a deconstructed temple—prismatic visions permeating an open colonnade that fall upon the interior in streams of incandescence from an accelerated sun.

Before the dancers activated this scene, an artist moved among the forms, building and rearranging their presence in her studio, measuring and altering their perception, formulating their dynamism. The set design enacts a gesture akin to the dancers' limbs; body and prop collapse into a single image that unfolds in a ceremony of abstraction. Light and environment become one—as material, as space, as performance.

. . .

In 1985, following a residency at the Capp Street Project in San Francisco, Barbara Kasten collaborated with the choreographer Margaret Jenkins on *Inside Outside/Stages of Light* at the Brooklyn Academy of Music in New York. It was the first time the artist's work was adapted for the stage. Over the course of the next four decades, subsequent exhibitions of her constructed environments in galleries and museums imparted viewers with the role of both performer and audience—collapsing the divided states of being inherent to theater into one continuous experience. In her studio, Kasten was always the first witness and subject—observing and manipulating how light transforms space as it is thrown upon and falls onto objects. At times, she photographed these settings to capture what was fugitive: the shape of light. This complex weaving, of how interactions with light alter our perception, has often been codified through the language of photography—a category that places a disproportionate attention on the medium (the record) used to capture the ephemeral (the work itself). Yet, a misreading of the conceptual constructions that have defined her phenomenological project since the 1970s has also excluded the spiritual nature of experience Kasten's work provokes.

In the context of art and architecture, the earliest works were devotional. Records from as early as 297 BCE claimed that the entirety of the world—adornments and the things that let them stand—existed in architecture as proof of divinity itself.[1] Ruins today stand as relics of a belief in gods. While religious sites have figured into Kasten's oeuvre, her travels to sites of ritual have deeply informed how she approaches the material used in her artistic

practice: light, space, color, and their communion. During her formative years as an artist, Kasten visited Le Corbusier's Ronchamp Chapel in 1965. As she writes in an essay published in *Art in America* in 2015, "the interplay of light, color and geometry at Ronchamp was a key inspiration as I developed my own artistic vocabulary."[2] In a similar moment of his career, Le Corbusier made a pilgrimage to visit the Parthenon in 1911. Decades later, in the commentary for his design of the Ronchamp Chapel (1950–55), he spoke of "infinite voices from the most distant centuries that reach today's most intense moments of modernity."[3] Kasten, recognizing the influence of Le Corbusier on Modernist architecture, reaches the contemporary via Antiquity in similar ways. Both are pilgrims who traveled in search of light. As Anne Carson writes of the pilgrim's ambitions beyond religion, "as you travel west, the days are longer: gold, more gold, and still more gold."[4] In search of this light, Kasten sought something of buildings that would allow her to decipher what ancient civilizations understood—that light determines form and, particularly in sacred structures, alters our perception of space and ourselves.

Certain scenes across time and space punctuate the history of Kasten's life and work. Encounters with the past provide insight into how, and why, she creates. In four acts that span the twentieth century, each spaced roughly thirty years apart, the scenes that compose this elective history have shaped, or been shaped by, her boundary-crossing practice. They envision an early feminist concept of historical lineage—one that is atemporal, cyclical, and subjective—yet remain united by encounters with architecture and spirituality. Against this backdrop, Kasten's return to the architectural basis of her work since 2015,

Barbara Kasten and Margaret Jenkins Dance Company, *Inside Outside/Stages of Light* (1985). Documentation of performance at the Brooklyn Academy of Music, Brooklyn, NY. Choreography: Margaret Jenkins. Costumes / Set Design: Barbara Kasten. Lighting: Sara Linnie Slocum with Barbara Kasten. Sound Score / Design: Bill Fontana. Courtesy of the artist

alongside her early engagement with archeological sites, evenly touches remnants of Antiquity and Modernism. Across each of Kasten's images and installations, we are bathed in a light that passes from the sacred to the material—to consecrate, as Le Corbusier did at Ronchamp, a phenomenon of light that exists as a marvel beyond religious aspiration. Here, in four parts.

. . .

SCENE I

The Caryatids Witness Le Corbusier
Athens, 1911

The gaze of the five caryatids remaining on the Porch of Maidens (stage left) are fixed upon the courtyard (opposite). Bodies carved in contrapposto—the delicate folds of their dresses more tensely draped across their outstretched legs—occupy a plinth upon the stage. The entablature that weighs upon their heads has stood for over two millennia; intricately braided hair gives strength to their necks to prevent them from snapping.

     The figure of a man (Le Corbusier) leans upon a fallen column. A single harsh light downstage center brightens the scene like the noontime sun.

     Clothed in a dark suit, the outline of his body appears indistinguishable from the tone of his silhouette. Shallow frames of marble slice through the landscape of the ruins, forcing a perspective shift as they move upstage.

     The Parthenon (out of view) is presumed behind the wing stage right.

The severity of the scene is composed of a body, an architectural relic, light, and its absence. Nothing more.

. . .

While Le Corbusier did not include columns within his architecture, it was his wandering through the Acropolis that led to his idea of the *promenade architecturale* (architectural promenade). A photograph of the architect taken in 1911—a black and white snapshot from his daily visits to the ancient site during his "Voyage d'Orient" to learn the fundamentals of architecture—shows him leaning against a fallen column in front of the Parthenon.[5] Visible at first approach from a diagonal, the Acropolis is entered from the far end of the structure. The architectural object must be navigated, absorbed before entering. This reversal, a method Le Corbusier recreated in the siting of his own work, made sense for the ancients. The conception of time in Greece during the Hellenic era was the product of a ritualistic frame of thinking that also extended to the placement of temples—as Roland Barthes writes, "the Greeks entered into Death backward: what they had before them was their past."[6] Nearly two decades before the completion of his *machine-à-habiter,* the Villa Savoye, Le Corbusier had compared the sequence of Grecian temples to a machine.[7] Though no clear statement on the nature of the architectural promenade exists, texts on the Villa La Roche designed alongside Pierre Jeanneret from 1923–25 come closest to describing its principals,

> You enter: the architectural spectacle at once offers itself to the eye. You follow an itinerary that allows space to develop with great variety, creating a play of light on the walls or making pools of shadow. Large windows open into perspectives of the exterior where the architectural unity is reasserted.[8]

An emphasis on the effects of architecture—how space is established, how we move among buildings, how shadows are cast—belonged to Le Corbusier's guiding logic as an architect. While these values resonate in Kasten's work, she is an artist that does not make buildings but instead responds to them. Her early interest in structures from Antiquity and sacred sites, completed alongside her characteristic geometric abstractions that she began in the 1970s, continue to inform how we read her ongoing experiments with light and space.

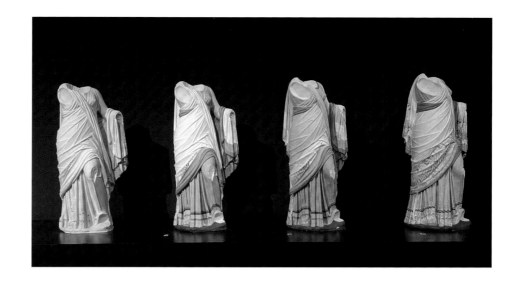

In Le Corbusier's extraction of Classical schemes, certain elements of ancient architecture once edited out by the Modernists, seen as inessential or decorative, are reincorporated and renewed in Kasten's interventions. Landing somewhere between the brutalist aesthetic of reinforced concrete and figurative embellishment of marble carvings, the forms that comprise Kasten's installations adhere to principles of both minimalism and structural ornamentation. In *Parallels I* (2017), a stack of fluorescent acrylic beams in red, blue, and yellow determine the space in a series of hollow but load-bearing supports. Amid the sculpture's translucent veils of color, which shift from primary into secondary and tertiary shades as you move around them, the edges of the piece appear electrically charged—the material catching, then concentrating, the ambient light of the space into sharp neon lines. Like the image of Le Corbusier leaning onto the fallen column, or the stone roof supported by the caryatids, as with nearly every example of Kasten's work, it is assembled and exists under the balance of its weight.

Balancing as a method of construction remains a trope in devotional and sacred architecture since at least the single-chamber tombs known as dolmen from the Neolithic period (4000–3000 BCE). A series of Kasten's cyanotypes of these "goddess architecture" sites, *Dolmen* (1991–94), feature images of temples and megalithic burial monuments across Turkey and France. In inverted hues of blue—the final image a negative due to the photographic process—the bodily presence of the stone and marble pillars appear at once X-ray-like and skeletal, spectral and vaporous. The cyanotype, the result of a chemical reaction of potassium ferricyanide and ferric ammonium citrate that develops when exposed to light, was invented by the astronomer Sir John Herschel in 1842. Later adopted by architects, it is where the term "blueprint" comes from.[9] Kasten's cyanotypes bear a relation to not only the scientific and formal, but also cultural and emotional implications of blue. Working at the turn of the twentieth century, the illustrations in mystic philosophers Annie Besant and C. W. Leadbetter's *Thought Forms* described all hues of blue as belonging to religious feeling—the rich deep color of "heartfelt adoration," the pale azure of "self-renunciation and union with the divine."[10] In his 1810 book *Theory of Colours*, Johann Wolfgang von Goethe writes, "we love to contemplate blue, not because it advances to us, but because it draws us after it."[11]

Blue belongs to the colorless (the sea), to ambience (the sky), and what is never reached (the mist of a mountain range that disperses as you approach). Across her cyanotypes, Kasten draws us into spaces of light through a hue that

Experimental color reconstructions of a statue of a marble statue of a Greek Muse in different stages by Vinzenz Brinkmann, Ulrike Koch-Brinkmann, and Bianca Kress. Installation view, *Bunte Götter: Die Farbigkeit Antiker Skulptur [Painted Gods: The Polychromy of Ancient Sculpture]* (2008). Courtesy of Liebieghaus, Frankfurt, Germany

often denotes distance in nature. In *Dolmen (La Roche-Aux Fées)* (1991), a lintel formed by a large boulder resting upon crude posts reveals a chamber. The perspective of the composition, which frames our gaze up towards the interior of the structure, is shared among Kasten's images of temples—we look to them from below. In Kasten, the blue of these ancient sites greets us with intimacy. Her images belong to a light that refuses to be lost.

The exception to the blue cast that envelops images of Kasten's sacred sites from this period is *Mané Rutual* (1994), a composite black and white image of various dolmen she photographed in Brittany, later conjoined into a single mural-scale panorama.[12] Glimmers of light passing through the gaps of the imperfect but solid stone, flares caused by the sun seeping through the tomb, are otherwise enmeshed in a grisaille of shadows. In Kasten's recent film installation *Sideways* (2015/2020), mapped upon the gallery walls in her 2020–21 solo exhibition *Scenarios* at the Aspen Art Museum, the dimensional quality of *Mané Rutual* is reprised. Featuring slivers of white projections—at times appearing as isolated inverted pyramids, at others like vertices of a folded screen—the video passes in a clockwise rotation across the space to create an atmosphere of interrupted light. In the reflection of the black terrazzo floors, the image of the film is doubled, placing the viewer within a false horizon of where the wall meets the ground. Geometry slowly encircles our vision. The same immersive space depicted within Kasten's 1994 mural envelopes us in light and its absence. In this disruption of scale, the gallery is transformed into a space where, in Kasten's words, "viewers disappear in the volume" or are otherwise absorbed "in the depth of the projected image."[13] In both works, we become imbricated by light.

In preparation for his unrealized "Theater of Totality"—an ambition that shares its desire with Kasten's installations to collapse performer and audience onto a single plane—the Bauhaus artist Láslzó Moholy-Nagy completed his *Light Prop for an Electrical Stage (Light-Space Modulator)* (1930). Devoid of recognizable markers of proportion to the body of the viewer, the constructivist nature and choreography of form in *Sideways* recalls the closely cropped passages of *Light Prop* captured in Moholy-Nagy's short film *Light Play: Black-White-Grey* from the same year. Throughout the 1930s— as a witness to the early years of the Nazi regime while in Germany—Moholy-Nagy's work with the Bauhaus was born of a firm opposition to a politics and culture that favored social regimentation over the collective. His ambitions to create, like Kasten, a tactile space unencumbered by the hierarchical division between the artist and the viewer sought to transform participation into

Mané Rutual (1994), archival lacquer jet spray on canvas. 8 × 25 feet (2.44 × 7.62 m). Courtesy of the artist

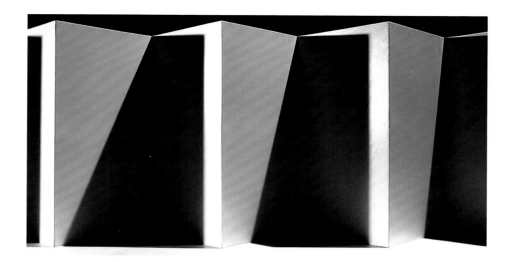

something more encompassing through abstraction. An ethos toward perception that could carry into life. For Moholy-Nagy, the traditional space of theater, which privileged the performer over the spectator, became a marker of fascism's favored social order. As with Kasten's recent film installations, *Light-Prop* sought to reject theatricality as "an articulated concentration of action derived from events and doctrines in their broadest meaning—that is to say, as 'dramatized' legend, as religious (cultist) or political promotion [...] to transmit an articulated experience."[14] This philosophical revolt, which extended to any institution that threatened the individual, spread to organized religion.

In the years leading up to *Light Prop*, fellow Bauhaus artist Lyonel Feininger made the woodcut *Cathedral of Socialism* (1919)—an image that circulated among members as an icon of the utopian possibilities of collective expression. Contrastingly, in the commission of the nighttime operated *Cathedral of Light (Lichtdom)* (1934–38) during the nascent years of the Nazi regime for the National Socialist Party's Nuremberg rallies, the monumental public installation by Hitler's principal architect Albert Speer pictured the possibilities of light as weapon.[15] Moholy-Nagy would have seen the fascist spectacle as he was developing *Light Prop*. While light remains a natural phenomenon, an energy transmitted from our closest star, its power is also harnessed for politics. In the drive to wield light as material, of abstraction as a replacement to representation, Moholy-Nagy and Kasten share the mythos of light as a source of liberation and dissolution of strict interpretation—a freedom of perspective necessary to abandon authority.

An experience of the sacred—that formless feeling that possesses no symbolic representation, that palpable experience we name the sublime—is an abstraction in itself. Le Corbusier's envisioning of light in at Ronchamp, or Kasten's recent installations, remain but few examples. While abstractions of light for the purposes of organized control did indeed belong to strategies of authoritarian reign, to enforce surrender over instinctual awe, the unraveling of representation in art exists beyond these bounds, and with inverse purpose. In the series *Hierophany* (1996), Kasten's most abstract cyanotypes from this period, the withdrawal from the image was forged by painting directly onto the paper with liquid chemicals that reacted to sunlight. Reminiscent of the cosmos, each composition was the result of how long they were exposed, how their pours pooled. The term "hierophany" is defined as any manifestation of the divine—a compound of the Greek adjective ἱερός (hierós), meaning "sacred," and the verb φαίνειν (phaínō), meaning "to reveal, to bring to light."[16] It

Stills from *Sideways* (2015/2020).
Courtesy of the artist

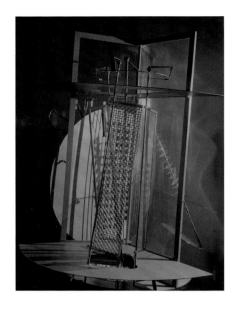

is the latter that Kasten delivers, and the materiality of light as a source of individual revelation she discloses.

. . .

SCENE II
The Sorcerer's Apprentice
Berlin / Chicago, 1936

The stage is divided in two by a curtain.

    Stage right: The Kroll Opera House is overtaken as Hitler delivers a speech before the Reichstag.

    Stage left: A replica of the Kroll Opera House with László Moholy-Nagy's set for *The Tales of Hoffmann* (1929) is reproduced at half-scale, dimly lit. The industrial and austere composition features a screen in the shape of an inverted pyramid that holds a pair of disembodied eyes, peering out onto the audience and the performers. The set looms like an echo, possessing the effect of a distant memory.

    Off-stage: a baby cries.

. . .

The year that Barbara Kasten was born, László Moholy-Nagy arrived in Chicago. Fleeing the early stages of Nazi rule in Berlin by way of London, with the help of Walter Gropius he was appointed the director of the New Bauhaus, later renamed the School of Design in 1939.[17] Though Kasten would not learn of her imminent proximity to Moholy-Nagy until she began her studies, their histories are intertwined. Born in the Chicago neighborhood of Bridgeport on the city's southside, Kasten's childhood home was mere steps away from what would become the future site of Moholy-Nagy's institution, hosted in Mies van der Rohe's Crown Hall, now part of the Illinois Institute of Technology's campus.

    In 2018, Kasten's *Artist/City (Crown Hall)* marked a return to interventions with the built environment, first explored in *Architectural Sites* (1986–89)—a series of elaborate, temporary nightlong installations within prominent museums. Inhabiting the interior of Mies's architecture, *Crown Hall* featured numerous metal tables affixed with broad sheets of fluorescent acrylic. Obliquely upturned and balancing upon one another, hues of red (which emits a bright pink), yellow

László Moholy-Nagy, *Lightplay: Black-White-Grey*,[17] (ca. 1926), gelatin silver print. 14.75 × 10.75 inches (37.4 × 27.4 cm). Gift of the artist. © 2022 Estate of László Moholy-Nagy. Courtesy of The Museum of Modern Art. Licensed by: SCALA/Art Resource, New York, NY

László Moholy-Nagy, stage set for *"Hoffmann's Erzählungen"* [*The Tales of Hoffmann*] (1929), by Jacques Offenbach (1819–80), Kroll-Opera Berlin. Photo: Lucia Moholy. 8 × 15 inches (21.2 × 38 cm). © akg-images. Courtesy of the Cologne Institute for Theatre Studies

(edges glowing an incandescent green), orange (burning the eyes like a construction vest), and blue (the softest of the suite, though still brilliantly intense) washed Mies's glass box with reflections and shadows of color. Against the diffused light of the frosted glass that divides the interior from the exterior of *Crown Hall*, Kasten's pulsating and dynamic installation achieved what the building alone did not: an undulation and softening of space that unfastened its famous rigidity and spare order.

From 1929 to 1931 Moholy-Nagy's avant-garde sets for the Kroll Opera House, then part of the Weimar Republic—including *Madame Butterfly*, *The Flying Dutchman*, and *The Tales of Hoffmann*—employed light as a sculptural element in productions toward similar means. The scenography encapsulated the artist's concept of "vision in motion," what historian Edit Tóth describes as "the magnification and doubling of the actor's gestures through the use of mirrors, shadows, and close-up film projection," to bring about "the interplay between theatrical distancing and intensification of embodied presence."[18] In Crown Hall, Kasten's transfiguration of space succeeded in staging the type of "total theater" envisioned by Moholy-Nagy; a merging of artist and audience likewise informed by her mentor Trude Guermonprez, a Bauhaus member she studied under during her time in California. As with Moholy-Nagy, Kasten's work in stage design in the 1980s helped to fuel her artistic practice, culminating in her collaboration with Postmodern choreographer Margaret Jenkins in *Inside Outside/Stages of Light* (1985). The stage, anticipated in sets Kasten began for the *Construct* series (1979–85), was replete with elements of moveable geometry—pyramids, pedestals, spheres, mirrors, and columns—structuring the bodies of the dancers for the audience through the same logic exercised in her studio. Both created, and were part of, the image.

Echoes of this gesture encompass *Scenario* (2015), first installed as part of *Stages* at the Graham Foundation in Chicago in 2015, and later in *Scenarios* at the Aspen Art Museum in 2020–21. A series of cubic forms, scattered upon the base of a constructed corner, whose backs and edges are left exposed to the viewer, are each painted an austere white. A video of scenes consisting of the same forms, rearranged and captured within the artist's studio, is projected at a larger scale directly onto the objects themselves. The light of the film, which acts as the primary agent of color, casts a secondary dimension of silhouettes that alter the geometry of the work in duotone hues of red/green, blue/aqua, orange/chartreuse, and yellow/ultramarine, among other combinations. Developing in front of us, the sculpture imparts an image in ways that a static photograph cannot. Throughout the 1980s and '90s the photographic documentation that resulted from the *Construct* series led to Kasten's classification as a Photographer, though her aims then were (and remain still) much more fluid than this designation allows. These images, what Kasten describes as "impossible landscapes,"[19] sought to arrest the behavior of objects in space in time. As attempts to capture the impermanence of the incidental photogram projected onto the wall through conditions of light, the images operate like film stills—static punctuations that record a larger narrative, however abstract.

The doubt of perception in installations such as *Scenario* or *Sideways* shares the aesthetic desire to not only suspend, but transform, understandings of space. Across the stage or the studio, Kasten's approach to *mise-en-scène* resists illusion in favor of manipulating subjective experience through interpretations of material. As polychromatic tensions that destabilize the built environment, the space activated by the projection of *Scenario* (white painted walls, white painted objects) is initially blank. The content of the work, which is to say its dimensionality, is primarily imbued by light. Across the marble ruins we now recognize as Classical architecture, we see a similar blankness. Yet these sites that were once host to ancient civilizations were painted in brilliant hues of red, emerald, and lapis; temples possessed mirror-like gilding on many of their elements (on columns, friezes, and borders); statues were embedded with gemstones for eyes. Time stripped them of color. In Kasten's film installations, their time-based element is what imparts their polychromy.

Barbara Kasten in her studio during the filming of *Scenario* (2015) in Chicago, IL. Courtesy of the artist and Art21

Scenario (2015). Installation view, *Stages*, Graham Foundation, Chicago, IL. Photo: RCH | EKH. Courtesy of the artist

A series of Polaroids, *Temples* (1996), offers a glimpse into Kasten's emerging color vocabulary: brilliant sunset violets and blues bleeding into atmospheres of diffuse orange and pink. Each photograph features a blurred outline of architectural shapes, apertures of columns and pillars. Scale here, too, is obscured—the shots may capture buildings from afar, edges dissolving from the breakdown of the camera zoom, or of models framed through the glass of museum vitrines. Neither source is revealed through the information the image discloses—the origin of the sites remains secreted. Inverting the expectations of how things should behave (in space, in front of the camera), Kasten confronts the bounds of representation. Though none of her images employ digital manipulation, each requires a type of faith—a way of seeing that can be trained and taught, instead of tricked. The reality Kasten presents is one that can be trusted, while also challenging how we see representation and form.

In the *Progression* series (2017–ongoing), geometric fragments of the same fluorescent material used in Kasten's sculptures and installations, such as *Parallels* or *Crown Hall,* are mounted upon the surface of a photograph. Refracting and emitting light like panes of stained glass, the works are composed by both an image of an object and its physical presence in space. Amid the square compositions, certain works appear elongated, almost rectangular, by virtue of the splinters of colored shadow that wash the surface of the image and pour onto the wall. What belongs to the photographic surface versus what belongs to the appendage upon the ground is left tenuous. Like *Scenario,* which manifests both the image (of form) and the counter-image (of projection), the advancement of each *Progression* destabilizes light and material to conceal the immediacy of its construction.

This suppression of perceptible knowledge, of what causes our understanding of the work, is a phenomenon intrinsic to Kasten's careful output. During Moholy-Nagy's time in Chicago at the School of Design, he too worked on subduing perception: in aiding the United States war effort, he developed camouflage.[20]

. . .

INTERMISSION
World War II

. . .

SCENE III
The Concrete Chapel
Ronchamp, 1965

Cue: fog machine (subtle).

The curtains draw to reveal a frontal barrier of fortified concrete blockading the stage. The mass of the wall is punctured by a modulated grid of windows, that cut through the obstruction—each inset with panes of different colored glass.

A severe light that slowly rotates on a mechanized arch from behind the hollow casts a sequence of polychromatic beams onto the audience as it passes through the apertures. Discernable illuminations trace through the air.

As eyes adjust, backlit symbols of hand-painted illustrations on the glass become more visible—outlines of birds, flowers, stars, moons, and clouds.

Changing shape as they pass over the house floor, the colored projections transform the seated bodies below into topographies of light. In concert with the artificial passing sun, the luminous cells wash over them in glows of crimson, green, gold, and blue.

. . .

"In a complete and successful work there are hidden masses of implications, a veritable world which reveals itself to those it may concern,"[21] writes Le Corbusier. In 1965, Kasten traveled to France for the first time to see the chapel designed by the Swiss architect in Ronchamp, commissioned following the bombing of the church that stood before World War II. The experience would become foundational to her early practice as a young artist.[22] Completing her undergraduate degree at the University of Arizona in 1959, Kasten found work through the cultural program of the United States Armed Forces and was employed for civilian service in Germany. While in Europe, she sought out architectural sites. "Bullet holes were still visible in walls," writes Kasten, "it became clear to me that architecture could embody both human atrocities and utopian aspirations."[23] In California while pursuing her graduate degree from California College of Arts and Crafts in Oakland, she studied under the Bauhaus textile artist Trude Guermonprez and in Poland with the sculptor Magdalena Abakanowicz. Kasten's first mature works—*Seated Forms* (1972) and *Figure/ Chair* (1973)—were informed by a newly attained mindset of architecture as a metaphor for human ideals and, perhaps, by what they left unmapped.

Temple III (1996), Polaroid. 24 × 20 inches (60.96 × 50.8cm). Courtesy of the artist

Kasten's pilgrimage to reach the Notre-Dame du Haut in Ronchamp did not begin with a religious desire. She was in Europe to work—though her motivation was guided by a secular, but no less revelatory aim: to travel, when she could, to spaces whose experience transcended physical encounters through light. The changeability of the Ronchamp Chapel, an interior of whitewashed concrete Kasten describes as an "otherworldly fantasy," divorced from principles of permanence in favor of a constant state of becoming, "as if I were in an intangible space, at once outside reality and deeply connected to the physical properties of light."[24] This elemental, fragmentary, and dynamic view of light and space shares a language of Cubism while attaining a phenomenological experience—how what we see, and how we see creates meaning. As Henry Plummer proposes in *Cosmos of Light*, a meditation on Le Corbusier's sacred sites, "Light is used to fracture forms, but more importantly to shatter conventions of realism and beauty, as it cuts up and rearranges things to introduce multiple perspectives, thereby altering the way we see and experience the world," presenting a realm that "encourages, even demands, that we become participants in shaping our own spiritual experience."[25] Across Kasten's immersive, glowing installations, like Le Corbusier's achievement at Ronchamp, her divinations of light internalize perception as thought beyond observation.

Kasten's most porous encounters with architecture take from Ronchamp their reliance upon an ever-shifting source—that of sunlight—to absorb and record how light passes through and within space. In *Crossover* (2016/2020), a film projected onto a narrow freestanding cycloramic wall, populated at its base with a series of open, cubic constructions of fluorescent acrylic, screens closer crops of the same configuration of objects in kaleidoscopic movements. What belongs to object, projection, or a shadow of its double is entangled—neither the static nor the simulated is privileged. The status of the work remains fractured while reaching a harmonious balance between image and

environment. In *Elevation* (2020), a site-specific installation commissioned by the Aspen Art Museum, designed by architect Shigeru Ban, a series of large-scale rose-hued mirrored panels installed along the corridor of the building reflect the glass exterior, which faces west. Shrouded in the woven grid of Ban's primary architectural motif—a warm wooden enclosure that wraps the museum against a landscape of often snow-capped mountains—the series of twelve panes are either mounted flush or suspended slightly from the wall in two standard depths. From noon to dusk, an ambient wash of the morning sun slowly turns to a starkly pronounced shadow as it passes through the architecture, enveloping the work in a cage of light. While no projector imparts media upon the sculpture, *Elevation* endures as a type of film—a lens that tracks the material reality of space and is "screened" for those who stand in front to find themselves reflected within. When viewed from a diagonal, only architecture and nature plays out—a vision that excludes the body.

In the 1889 publication *Histoire de l'architecture* (*History of Architecture*), architectural historian Auguste Choisy conceived of what became an apocryphal reasoning to the understanding behind the diagonal positioning of Classical buildings in ancient Greece. Examining the Acropolis as a case study for his proposal of the *pittoresque*, frontality was described as "an exception that always had a particular motive."[26] For Choisy, the Greek usage of oblique sightlines controlled a purposeful counter to monumentality, an approach that presented an optical tableau favorable to the "cold alignments" of Beaux-Arts architecture.[27] However unfounded, Choisy's claims—a fantasy of "scenery" that contradicted surviving Greek legal documents of how the placement of temples were the product of a ritualistic system of belief among the ancients related to their theories of afterlife, which he scrutinized and later ignored—became part of an architectural history that later influenced Le Corbusier. The rule of lateral perspective and anti-frontality became a hallmark of the intentional siting of his projects, including the placement of the Ronchamp Chapel.

The asymmetrical siting of temples has inspired Le Corbusier and Kasten alike—a dynamic approach to alignment that remains an essential device in both their work. Choisy's conception of the *pittoresque* abides by an attitude toward the built environment that hinges upon a response to what is already there; a completion of harmony that elaborates on what cannot be moved and must be contended with. It is through this logic that Kasten's 1980s series *Architectural Sites* altered the understanding of buildings—upending expectations of static matter by injecting interiors with mirrors, casting specific temperatures of light

Shigeru Ban Architects, Aspen Art Museum (2014), Aspen, CO. © Michael Moran / OTTO, Derek Skalko

Elevation (2020), mirrored acrylic. 105 × 208 ½ × 5 ⅛ inches (266.7 × 529.6 × 13 cm). Installation view, *Scenarios*, Aspen Art Museum, Aspen, CO. Photo: Simon Klein. Courtesy of the artist

to confuse frontal and receding space, and inserting geometric forms to flatten and obscure dimensionality. One decade later, in the mid-1990s, Kasten's cyanotypes of temples throughout the Aegean coast of Greece and Turkey pictured a series of architectural relics. Like the light achieved in the *Architectural Sites,* Kasten's *Gumuskesen (Turkish Temples)* (1995) pictures an interior that appears to radiate against the silhouette of a colonnade. Both bodies of work subvert how light behaves—intensity where one would expect shadows, and conversely, depth where one would expect the brilliance of a façade.

The appearance of temples across Kasten's work from the 1990s reach toward the spiritual potential of architectural abstraction that carries into her recent sculptures and installations. Abandoning the confines of representing buildings, and instead staging the elements that react to the built environment, Kasten's erasure of the limits between object and light enact Le Corbusier's concept of *espace indicible* (ineffable space)—"miracle" marked by a "boundless depth [that] opens up, effaces the walls, drives away contingent presences."[28] Whereas Le Corbusier made use of ancient sites in their comparison to the machine—to industry and modernity—Kasten's work bridges the simplification of Mid-Century architecture with the mystic properties of devotional sites. A transubstantiation between image and form, whose transcendental quality is characteristic of her work from the cyanotypes to the present. In her evocations of light, Kasten reaches back to touch the elements of spirit in Antiquity and brings them closer to us.

. . .

SCENE IV

Museum of Underwater Archeology
Bodrum, 1995

A moonlit scene.

Center stage: an orb emitting a sharp silver light is suspended above the scenery. The courtyard of a temple, framed by columns, is bathed in a soft blue hue from the outer reaches of the stage.

Props of vessels are scattered among the ground—plaster replicas of amphorae spaced unevenly across an expanse of packed earth. Each individual form lays upon a crisp carpet of paper. As time progresses, the space surrounding the outline of their shadows transforms into a dark azure, developing on the surface like the depths of the sea.

The white apparitions cast by the silhouettes of the vases are best visible from the balcony.

. . .

Fluorescence and moonlight occupy opposite poles of perception—one assaults the senses, while the other soothes. Both sources of light have figured into Kasten's method of describing objects in space, across experiments from the mid-1990s to more recent installations from 2015 to 2020. The phenomenologist philosopher Maurice Merleau-Ponty argued that the architectural task was "to make visible how the world touches us," to create structures that evoke an embodied metaphor for being in the world.[29] In Kasten's practice, which continues to evolve up to the present moment, this point of contact enters our bodies through the extremities of perception to affect how we conceive creations of space. More than any other point of her career, the 1990s saw a proliferation of ancient material in Kasten's work. From architecture to artifacts, the cyanotype—like Moholy-Nagy's photogram— served as her gateway into abstraction. Following the lineage of Kasten's work with sacred sites and devotional objects, the subject of her current installations questions not only how we see, but also how we feel, how we relate to one another, the world around us, and our place within it. Abstraction has never existed without consequence. For Moholy-Nagy, both in visual terms and in practice, the withdrawal from representation positioned a revolt to authoritarian thought, to the oppression of the individual, toward a more harmonious vision of Modern life. In Kasten's ritual engagement with light and form, her work imparts these same ideals toward a contemporary context.

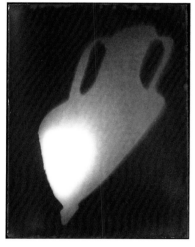

Amphora (Knidos) (1996), cyanotype. 30 × 22 inches (76.2 × 55.8 cm). Photo: Thomas A. Nowak. Courtesy of the artist

In the mid-1960s, deep-sea divers off the southern Aegean coast discovered a shipwreck 36–42 meters below the surface, which dated to the late Roman period from the fourth to fifth centuries CE. There, they excavated several amphorae—ancient vessels that would become part of the collection of the Sualtı Arkeoloji Müzesi (Museum of Underwater Archeology) in Bodrum, Turkey. Participating in a residency there, Kasten encountered these objects and made cyanotypes of their silhouettes by moonlight in the courtyards of the neighboring temples. Kasten's *Amphora* (1995–96) marked a return to images in blue, twenty years after the artist's *Photogenic Paintings* (1973–75). Encouraging the sublime of the quotidian, the 1970s compositions—crafted from the shadows of tightly cropped expanses of factory-produced screening material (the kind inserted into the panes of windows and doors)—rippled upon the surfaces of the photograph like waves. Denying allusions to landscape, the silhouette of works such as *Amphora (Rhodes)* (1996) initiate a gestalt effect that triggers recognizable forms that are often figurative, materializing like fragments of portraiture or bodies. Across each of Kasten's *Amphora*, the imprint of the vessels' elongated shadows brought into being via the cyanotype process impart a softened understanding of their form. Once used as objects of containment, both ceremonial and utilitarian, their flattened volume further abstracts the history of their purpose—instead, Kasten's exposures return to their origin of discovery. The edges between the outline of the amphora and the negative space of the ground dissolve into one another as if underwater, like glimmers upon an ocean floor. Whereas Kasten's *Dolmen* (1991–94) and *Temples* (1995–96) were exposed during the day, what differentiates the *Amphora* from related images during the same period remains their reliance on moonlight.

The moon is a female archetype, as is the sea. Both are interdependent in nature; the waxing and waning cycle of the one causes the other to swell and recede. The personification of each belongs to the vast and enigmatic—to beauty, but also to danger and mutability. As emblems of goddess figures, of fertility, the guises of celestial and marine forces in mythology, literature, and art pose an antithesis to the linearity of patriarchal thought, the illusion of the knowable. In collective consciousness, this gendering of nature operates as a symbolic portent of the extremities between regeneration and destruction. Histories of civilizations seem to have agreed that the contemplations and activities of women take place in the shadows. Within this context, Kasten's *Amphora* brings the presence of the vessel's volume into being through light—focusing on its form as its substance, not its ability to contain another. This gesture holds Kasten's perhaps most feminist ideal; a paradigm that allows form to exist without the expectation of what it must carry (as content, as meaning) to be valid. Across decades, her work exacts the permission of abstraction.

The harsh boundaries that so often divide how space ought to perform is diminished under the modulated conditions of Kasten's recent installations, where extremities of matter and atmosphere are permeable, their oppositions softened. Manufacturing the sensorial impact of light to destabilize what constitutes our tactile and visual reality persists in Kasten's work today, as it has since the 1970s, solidified in her cyanotypes from the 1990s. The impact of the artist's recent installations owes this history not only to their relationship to photography, but to her early study of sacred sites. The constructivist nature of how interventions such as *Crown Hall* or *Elevation* consider place is nascent in her approach to recording cavities and chambers forged by human hands to hold the things important to us (honorific goods, the dead) through building. This attitude toward space—established across Kasten's installations within architectural sites, namely museums and institutions—responds to the changeable character of the structures that survive us. How sunlight filters into the voids of ancient relics, how moonlight falls to capture the contour of vessels—how in looking at each of these things at different times of day our perspective of edifices and objects shift, slowly accruing a fuller understanding with each observation.

While many of the ancient and prehistoric locations Kasten photographed throughout the 1990s were scattered across Europe, in the United States she looked West. Two images from the *Puye Cliff Dwellings* (1990) series picture the roofs of the Indigenous site once home to 1,500 Pueblo Indians from ca. 900 to 1580 CE.[30] The companion images *New Mexico (The Ruins)* and *New Mexico (The Place)* capture the landscape in projections of blue light upon the cliff face and mesa top. In the former, a frontally composed aerial view of the over thousand-year-old brick dwellings features a glimpse of a diagonal horizon line in the upper left corner. If not for this feature, the image would appear as a surface marked by shallow, meandering lines—labyrinthine and diagrammatic. In its counterpart, a print depicting a detail of one of the dwellings' openings, the exterior of the subterranean space is transformed into a scenographic atmosphere cast by the gel of a theater light positioned off-camera. A wooden ladder descends into the hollow, ominous if not for the warm light emitting from beneath the cavern against the cold suffusion of the foreground. In both images, Kasten constructs trials of flatness and depth that displace our understanding of the dwellings as vacant—in recording the spaces through adaptation, the landscape holds the imprint of history, inhabited by light.

Across Kasten's conceptual approach to light as material, the spatial aura exacted within these meditations in blue from the 1990s remains fundamental to the perception of her varied chromatic installations and films since 2015. Grafting the ways in which Kasten's images of sacred sites capture space onto her present installations permits a reading of the artist's phenomenological approach to abstraction—ephemeral intimations that make visible how the world touches us. As light that passes through architecture, both manufactured and altered in Kasten's work, its dispersions, edges, and shadows build an understanding of the same moments that once led to the building of ritualistic sites centuries ago. In place of the singular and outlasting, her work persists in a series of monuments to light whose changeability is constant—mutable iterations of form and atmosphere composed for the unknown bodies that will encounter them. To move through space and see how light touches us differently: this is their architecture. The body of the artist, that original vessel of the performance, completes this journey first—from the building of the stage to curtain close, of records left in shadows.

[1] Clemente Marconi, "Kosmos: The Imagery of the Archaic Greek Temple," *Anthropology and Aesthetics*, no. 45 (Chicago: The University of Chicago Press, 2004), 211.
[2] Barbara Kasten, "Architectural Light," *Art in America*, 2015.
[3] From *Textes et dessins pour Ronchamp*. J. K. Birksted, *Le Corbusier and the Occult* (Cambridge: The MIT Press, 2009), 40.
[4] Anne Carson, *Plainwater* (New York: Vintage, 1995), 183–84.
[5] Daniel Sherer, "Le Corbusier's Discovery of Palladio in 1922 and the Modernist Transformation of the Classical Code," *Perspecta*, vol. 35 (Cambridge: The MIT Press, 2004) pp. 20–39. Here 22.
[6] Roland Barthes, *Camera Lucida: Reflections on Photography* (New York: Hill and Wang, 2010), 71. Originally published as *La Chambre Clair*, trans. Richard Howard (Paris: Éditions du Seuil, 1980).
[7] Wayne R. Dynes, "Medievalism and Le Corbusier," *Gesta*, vol. 45, no. 2 (Chicago: The University of Chicago Press on behalf of the International Center of Medieval Art, 2006), 92.
[8] Le Corbusier and Pierre Jeanneret, *Œuvre Complète 1910–1929* (Zurich: Les Éditions d'Architecture Artemis, 1946), 60. Translation by the author.
[9] Courtney Reed, "From blue skies to blueprint: Astronomer John Herschel's invention of the cyanotype," *Ransom Center Magazine*, 2010.
[10] Annie Bessant, C. W. Leadbeater, *Thought Forms* (London: The Theosophical Publishing House, 1901), 44.
[11] Johann Wolfgang von Goethe, *Theory of Colours*, trans. Sir Charles Eastlake (London: John Murray, 1840), passage 781. Originally published in 1810.
[12] In the early 1990s, the Adobe and Apple corporations sponsored a program for artists during the development of the first Photoshop software. Kasten was one of the participants, which allowed her to composite this work.
[13] Kasten, "Architectural Light," 2015.
[14] Joyce Tsai, "The Sorcerer's Apprentice: László Moholy-Nagy and His *Light Prop for an Electrical Stage*," *In Reconsidering the Total Work of Art*, eds. Anke Finger and Danielle Follett (Baltimore: Johns Hopkins University Press, 2010), 286.
[15] The *Light Cathedral* was generated by over a hundred of the most advanced anti-aircraft searchlights, which Albert Speer had requisitioned directly from the Luftwaffe's reserves. Tsai, "The Sorcerer's Apprentice," 298.
[16] The term was popularized by the noted scholar of comparative religion, Mircea Eliade (1907–86).
[17] The Moholy-Nagy Foundation, moholy-nagy.org/chronology.
[18] Edit Tóth, "Capturing Modernity Jazz, Film, and Moholy-Nagy's *Light Prop for an Electric Stage*" (*Modernism/Modernity* 22, no. 1, 2015), 23–55.
[19] Kasten, "Architectural Light," 2015.
[20] The Moholy-Nagy Foundation, moholy-nagy.org/chronology.
[21] Birksted, *Le Corbusier and the Occult*, 145.
[22] Le Corbusier's iconic church, the Chapel of Notre Dame du Haut (Ronchamp, 1950–55), was one of three religious sites he designed in France throughout the 1950s and '60s, including the Monastery of Sainte Marie de la Tourette (Éveux-sur-l'Arbesle, 1953–60), and the posthumously constructed Church of Saint-Pierre (Firminy-Vert, 1960–2006).
[23] Kasten, "Architectural Light," 2015.
[24] Ibid.
[25] Henry Plummer, *Cosmos of Light: The Sacred Architecture of Le Corbusier* (Indiana: University of Indiana Press, 2013), 14.
[26] Birksted, *Le Corbusier and the Occult*, 85.
[27] Ibid.
[28] Birksted, *Le Corbusier and the Occult*, 306.
[29] David Seamon, "Merleau-Ponty, Perception, and Environmental Embodiment: Implications for Architectural and Environmental Studies," *Carnal Echoes: Merleau-Ponty and the Flesh of Architecture* (Journal for Social Sciences, vol. 6 no. 6, 2018), 5.
[30] The Pueblo Indians were ancestors of the Santa Clara people, who now reside at Santa Clara Puebla, 10 miles east of the Puye Cliff Dwellings in the Rio Grande River Valley.

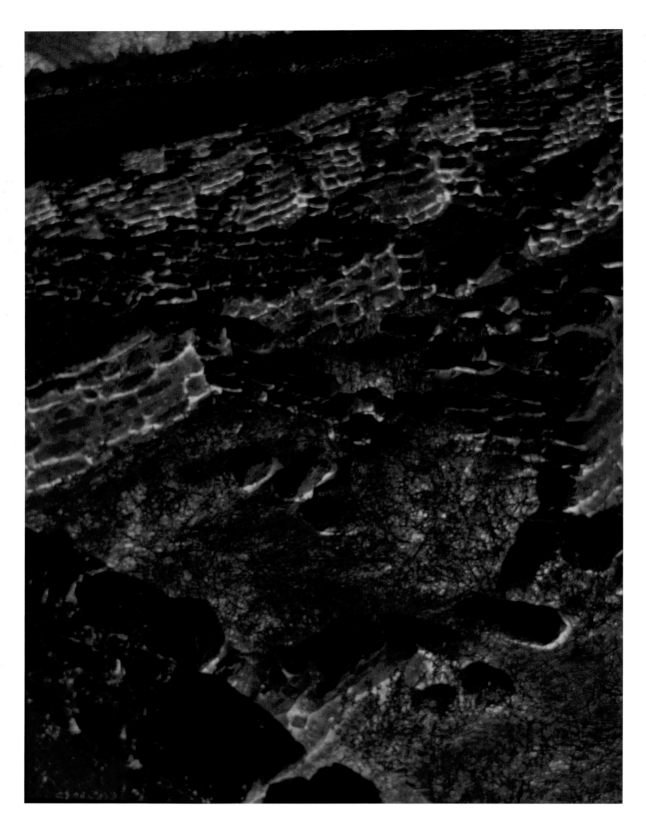

Puye Cliff Dwellings, New Mexico (The Ruins) (1990), cibachrome. 40 × 30 inches (101.6 × 76.2 cm). Courtesy of the artist

Puye Cliff Dwellings, New Mexico (The Place) (1990), cibachrome. 40 × 30 inches (101.6 × 76.2 cm). Courtesy of the artist

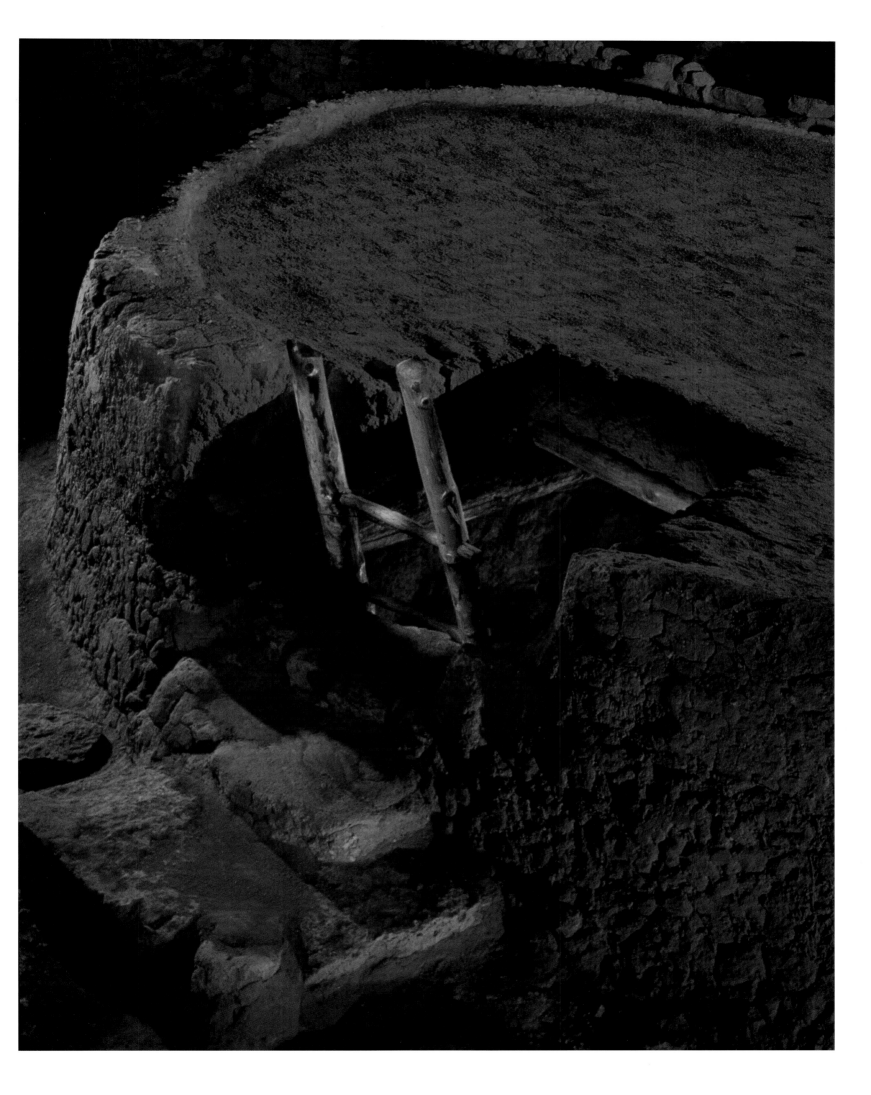

Dolmen (La Roche aux Fées) (1991),
cyanotype.
40 × 30 inches (101.6 × 76.2 cm).
Photo: Thomas A. Nowak. Courtesy
of the artist

Dolmen (De Crocuno) (1991), cyanotype.
40 × 30 inches (101.6 × 76.2 cm).
Photo: Thomas A. Nowak. Courtesy
of the artist

Turkish Temples (Temple of Zeus)
(1995), cyanotype.
22 × 30 inches (55.8 × 76.2 cm).
Photo: Thomas A. Nowak. Courtesy
of the artist

Barbara Kasten 1995

Amphora (Rhodes) (1996), cyanotype.
Two panels; 60 × 22 inches (152.4 × 55.8 cm).
Photo: Thomas A. Nowak. Courtesy
of the artist

Following pages

Amphora (Knidos) (1996), cyanotype.
30 × 22 inches (76.2 × 55.8 cm).
Photo: Thomas A. Nowak.
Courtesy of the artist

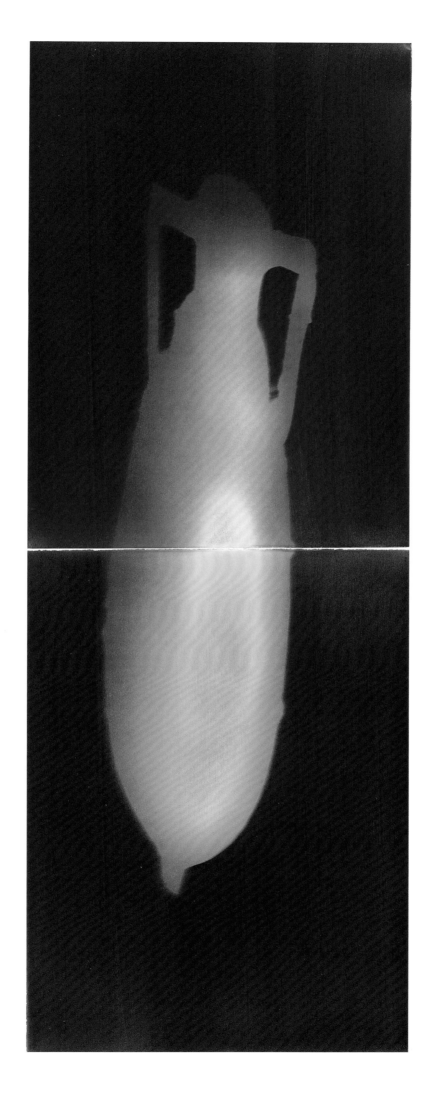

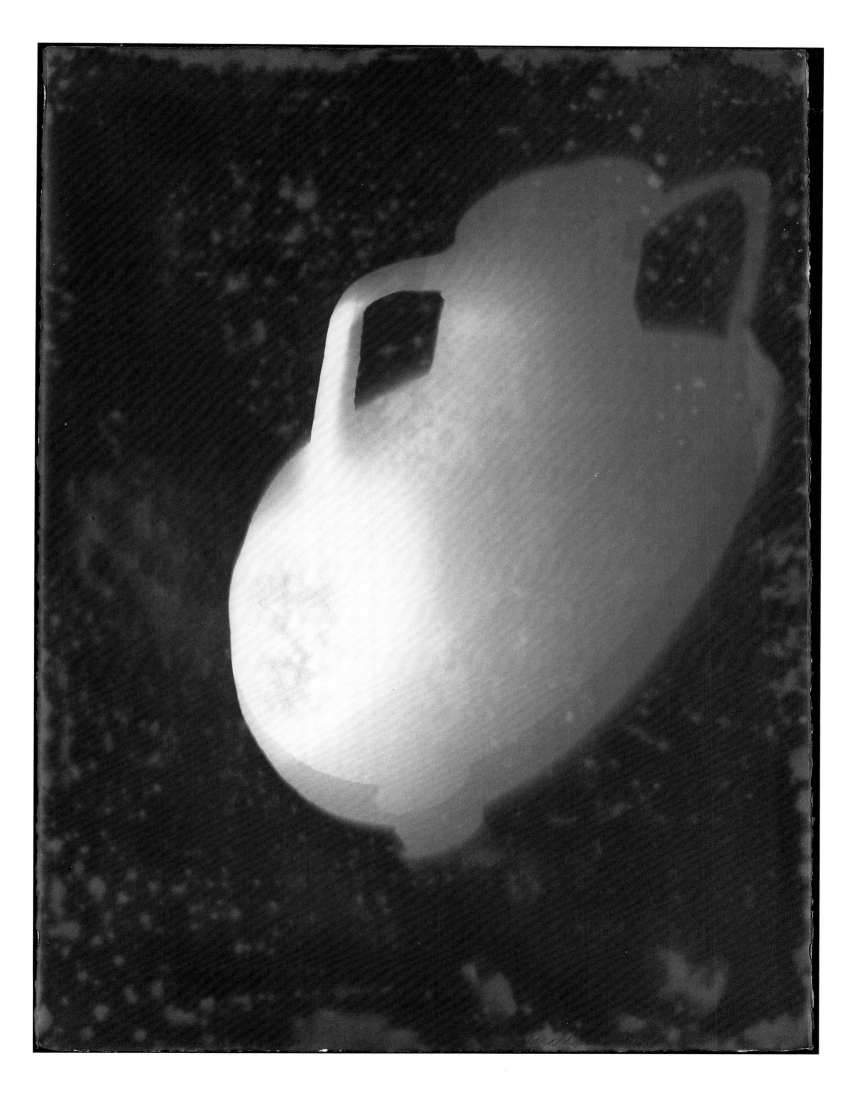

Amphora (Double Exposure) (1995),
cyanotype. 30 × 22 inches (76.2 × 55.8 cm).
Photo: Thomas A. Nowak.
Courtesy of the artist

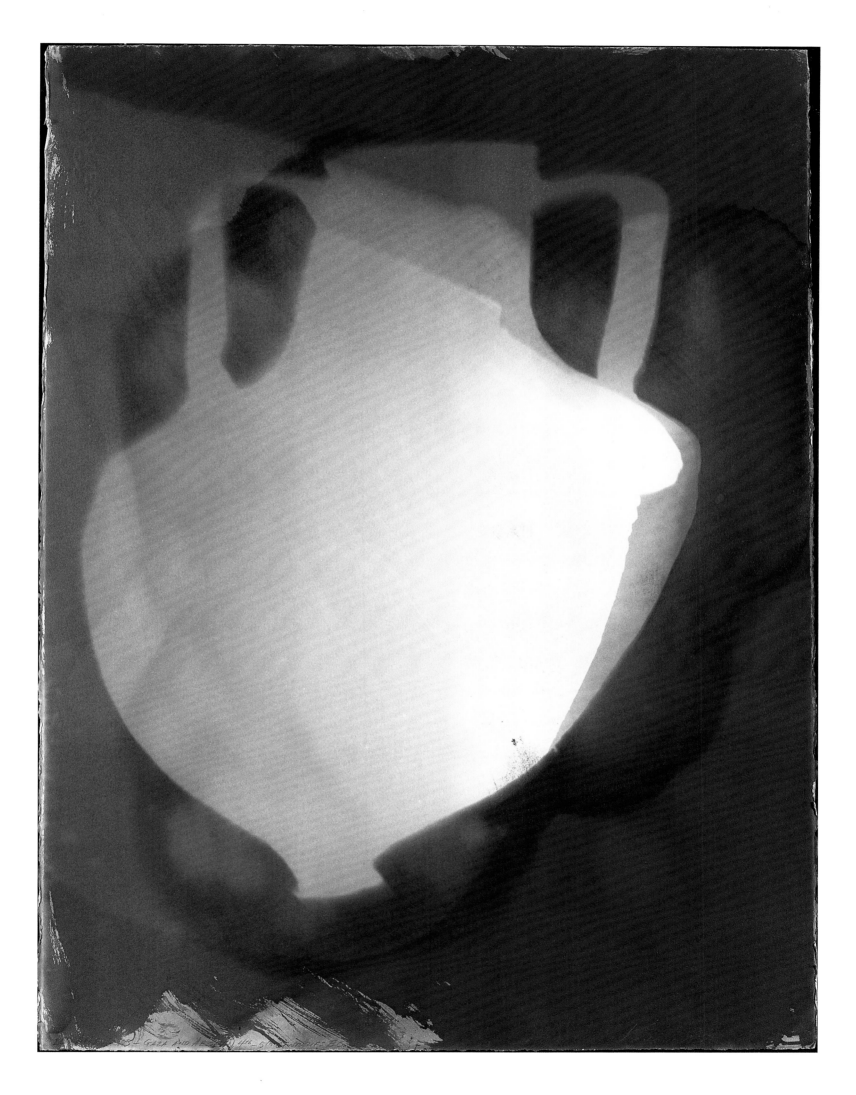

Hierophany VII (1996), cyanotype.
30 × 22 inches (76.2 × 55.88 cm).
Photo: Thomas A. Nowak. Courtesy
of the artist

Following pages

Hierophany XIV (1996), cyanotype.
30 × 22 inches (76.2 × 55.88 cm).
Photo: Thomas A. Nowak. Courtesy
of the artist

Hierophany XVIII (1996), cyanotype.
30 × 22 inches (76.2 × 55.88 cm).
Photo: Thomas A. Nowak. Courtesy
of the artist

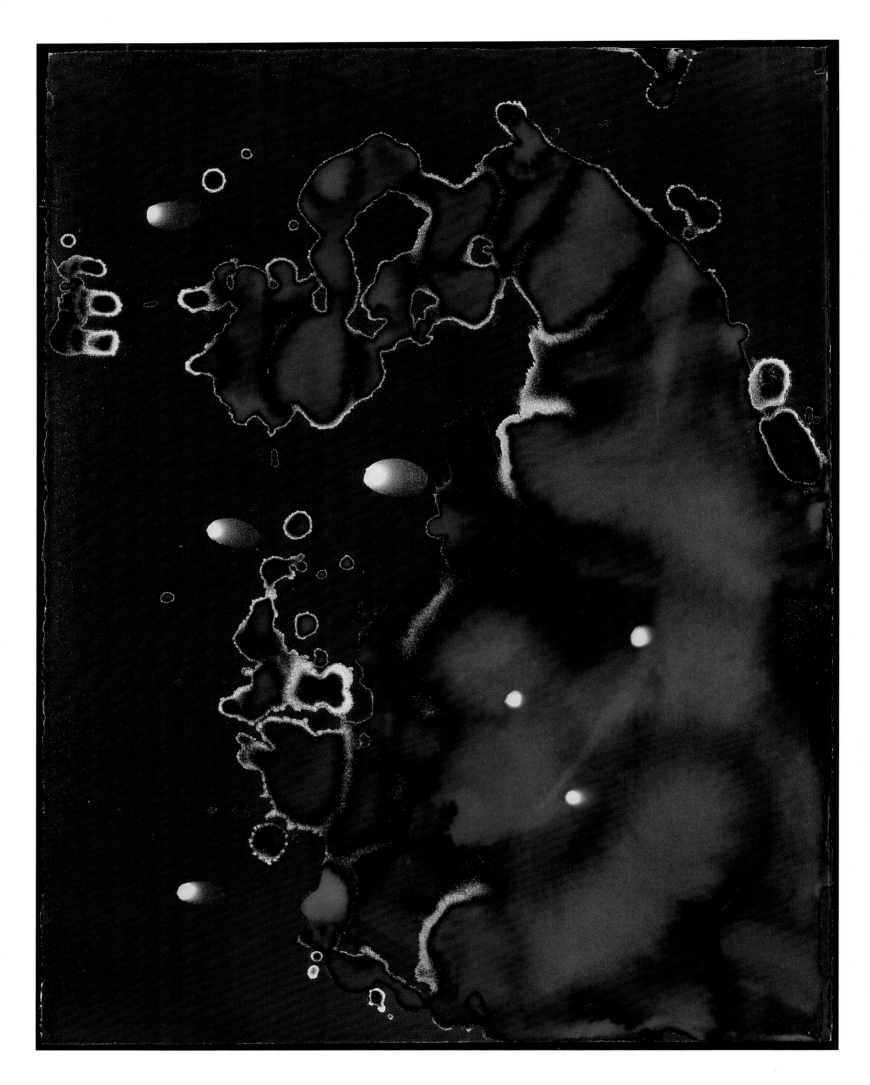

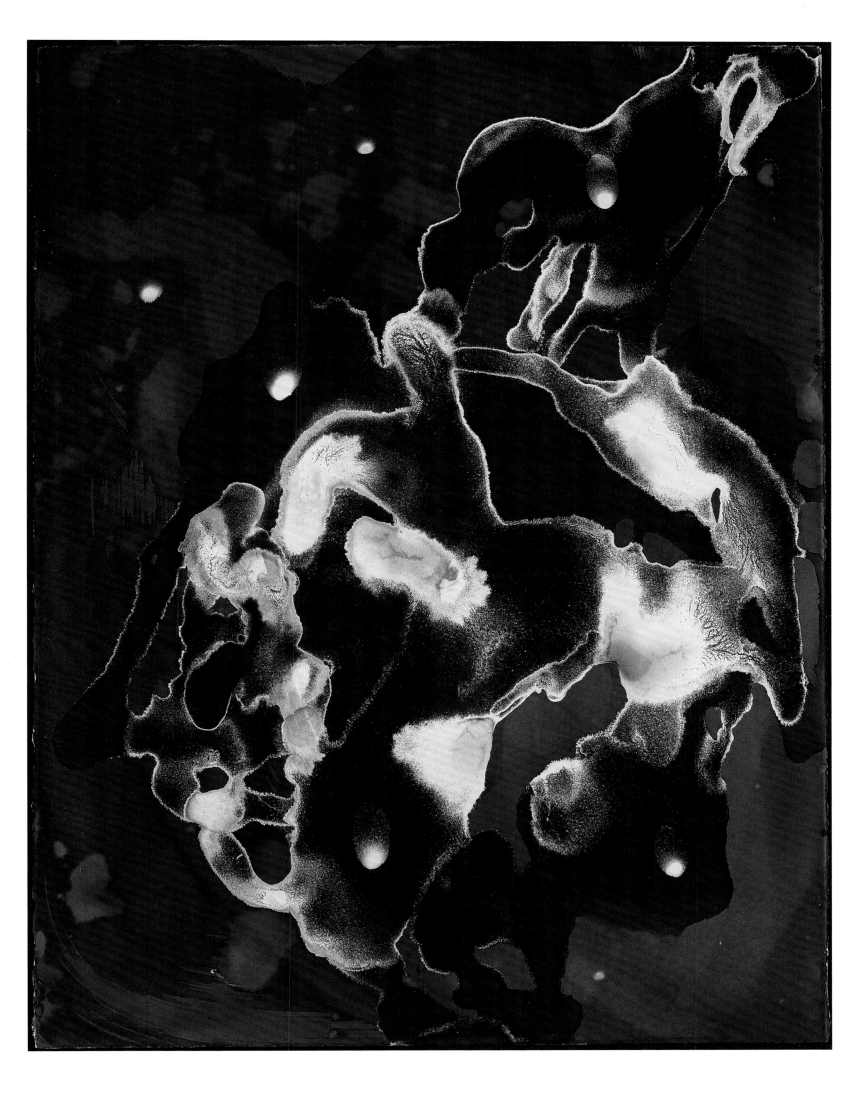

Hierophany XXVII (1996), cyanotype.
22 × 30 inches (55.88 × 76.2 cm).
Photo: Thomas A. Nowak. Courtesy
of the artist

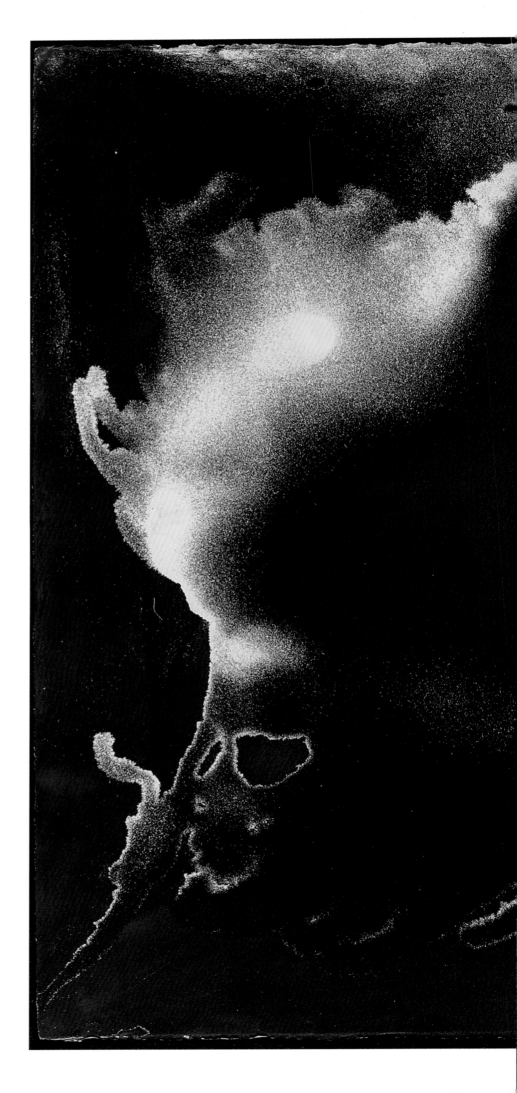

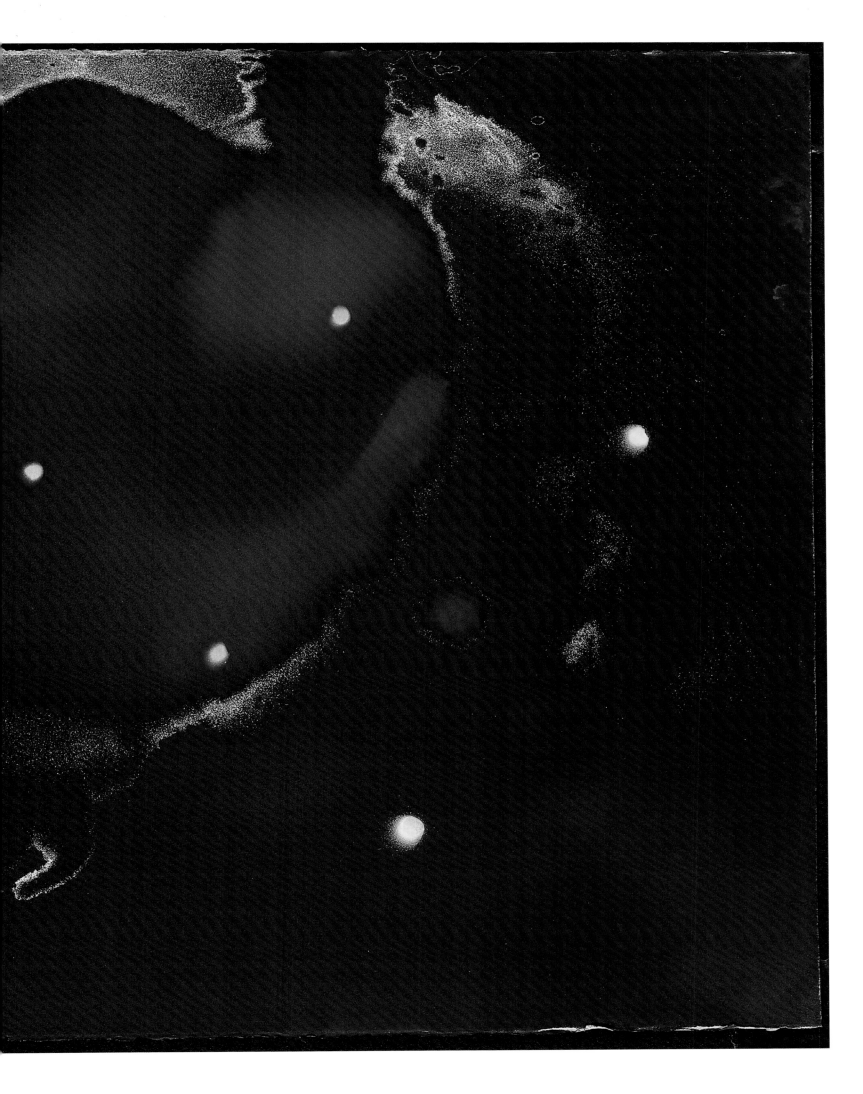

Towards an Emotional Architecture

Humberto Moro

I. L. Barragán

In the spring of 1976, the architect Luis Barragán began the construction of one of his masterpieces and final work: the Casa Gilardi in Mexico City. Commissioned by advertising executive Francisco Gilardi, the house was planned as a residency upon a rather small plot of land, already surrounded by buildings on three sides.[1] The house is a modest space in both scale and scope compared to the architect's better-known projects, such as the Cuadra San Cristóbal, the Satellite Towers, or the Casa Prieto López. The bright pink façade of Casa Gilardi is situated in the midst of a traditional, upper-middle-class neighborhood. This house is where Barragán allowed himself to exercise color, surface, and light, arguably like nowhere else, establishing an anomaly within the architect's work insofar as color—not space, nor scale—takes center stage.

The house—which remains a residence and has been preserved unchanged up until to today (it is open to the public by appointment)—is composed of distinct emblematic spaces that revolve around different color parameters. A jacaranda tree, with its beautiful lilac flowers, was already living in the plot—in fact, a first draft of the house included a heavy presence of the muted violet tone of the tree's flowers as part of many of the interior's perspectives.[2] The presence of the tree served as both an inspiration and a challenge for the architect, who decided to design the spaces of the house around it. The patio, where the tree still grows, allows light into a long hallway from a line of thin, rectangular windows. The yellow light that seeps through the vertical portals virtually determines any other experiences of the space. Separated by a double door, the hallway leads into a formal dining room space, which holds one of the main features of the house—an indoor pool that marks the far end of the building. The pool is delineated by a clean play of shapes and colors: two opposite corners—one white wall occupies the right, a saturated blue on the left—that is intersected by a single magenta barrier, which emerges from the water and meets the ceiling.

Barragán has spoken about this signature element in different ways. Sometimes, covertly: "I will tell you a secret: the pool has a wall or a pink column which does not bear anything. It is a piece of color situated in the water."[3] On other occasions, with great clarity of what the wall itself achieved: "That column in the middle of the pool goes against all rules, however, it is there because it needed to be there, for space to be defined, to allow the play of light and include a color in the composition."[4] In this sense, one of the most critical elements of the composition was not functional, but necessary for the interaction with space and light.

Barragán was led to color by grace of the space: "I use color, but when I draw, I am not thinking about it. Regularly, I define color when the space is already built. I visit at different times of the day and begin to 'imagine color;'

I think about a range of colors that go from the most daring, up to the most credible."[5] Barragán's methodical approximation to color was a result of a plastic process, whereby he would make "models in cardboard to create volumes, leaving white masses and adding black pieces of various proportions" so as to allow himself to play with black and white as "absolute opposites" and to find different relationships between them.[6] But it was also the result of a rigorous exploration of the physical space, in the awareness of environmental attributes of the space itself—such as the color of the blossoms of the trees nearby, the spaces into which the sunlight entered at certain times of the day, as well as the composition and plastic elements of his own work. But above all, he was aware of, and resisted, a prevailing academicism in architecture. He called himself an "anti-academic architect."[7]

There is a bricolage of influences in Barragán's work; he spoke about beauty, the influence of plastic (visual) arts—of serenity,[8] silence, and the soothing influence of religious spaces. At the same time, he also spoke about the volumes of precolonial architecture alongside elements in vernacular colonial spaces, and the nostalgia of rural Mexico.[9] The interchangeability of how he used these terms allowed for certain opacity. While individual influences remain difficult to reconcile, each are concretely felt within the work. Among Barragán's output, one senses how the transformation of materials allows for possibilities that transcend formal categories of our physical world.

Barragán often used the term "emotional architecture" to describe how he worked with the formal elements of line, color, planes, and scale in active dialogue with environmental aspects such as light (and in this case, a jacaranda tree) to convey a sensation both through and within space. "It is very important for humankind that architecture should move them with its beauty; if there are many equally valid technical solutions to a problem, the one which involves a message of beauty and emotion—that is architecture."[10] This newly coined term, emotional architecture, as an explanation of his oeuvre would affect generations to come: a transformation of materials into an experience so strong that it destabilized the very nature of matter, human perception, and all things physical. A "transubstantiation."[11] Is the water in the pool really water, or a mirror? Is the light in the hallway passing from the outside, or is its vibrancy imparted by the color of the interior walls?

No description I can write is, or could be, a substitute for witnessing what Barragán creates of space.

II. B. Kasten

Barbara Kasten has never been motivated to "push the boundary of photography."[12] Since the 1970s, she has used the medium as a vehicle to achieve something foreign to the medium itself: an experience of space. "You experience a moment because you are there," says Kasten, "but people do not necessarily read photography as experiential."[13] Her refusal to fall into any artistic category dictated by the medium, material, or by any virtuous use of either has determined her tireless exploration towards the potential of light and space both in and around images. Throughout her career, Kasten's work denotes a shift from the representation of space to the creation and the transformation of space. Instead, the artist captures "the perceptual phenomena that she witnesses through the camera lens."[14] Kasten's approach situates the environmental and experiential—the spatial—at the center of her practice. The influence of her work and its ongoing dialogue with architecture

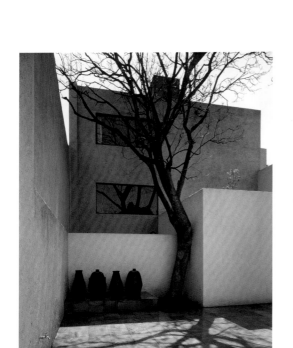

Luis Barragán (1902–1988), Gilardi House, Mexico City, 1975–77. View of the central patio (undated photograph, ca. late 1970s). Photo: Armando Salas Portugal. © Barragan Foundation, Switzerland / ProLitteris, Zurich

Luis Barragán (1902–1988), Gilardi House, Mexico City, 1975–77. Swimming pool access (undated photograph, ca. late 1970s). Photo: Armando Salas Portugal. © Barragan Foundation, Switzerland / ProLitteris, Zurich

Luis Barragán (1902–1988), Gilardi House, Mexico City, 1975–77. Swimming pool with free-standing wall (undated photograph, ca. late 1970s). Photo: Armando Salas Portugal. © Barragan Foundation, Switzerland / ProLitteris, Zurich

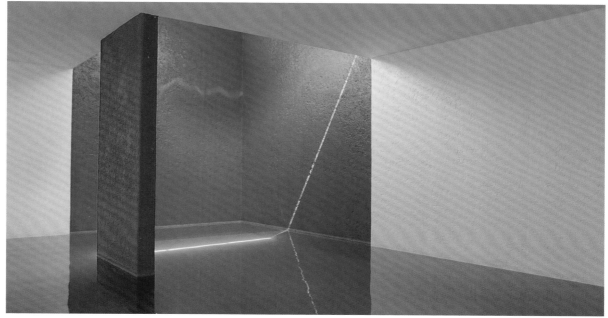

is critical. Not only because the artist's spatial awareness connects directly with her process and intention, but also because this relationship prevents the historical misplacement or material misunderstanding of the work.

One of Kasten's first images of a built set, *Construct I B* (1979), a 10 × 8 Polaroid photograph, depicts a composition of black, white, transparent, and mirrored surfaces. Each is activated by light—the shadows cast by the objects themselves create myriad forms that trace its trajectories. Partial objects are reflected; thin lines of what appear to be wire form a diagonal pattern. Upon closer inspection, the tension of the intimate and concentrated composition is revealed as being contained within a small, squared mirror that centrally connects the geometric elements.

Starting around 1979 and up until 1986 Kasten would produce the *Construct* series, which join this intricate composition of and within space. Through colored surfaces, stage lights, shapes, and shadows, the artist's images of space were not preoccupied with ideas of place, but instead evocatively pictured sensations of an environment. These life-size stage sets, like tableaux, began with Kasten's body moving through the studio and experiencing the volumes and reflections while she was assembling them. Ultimately, the goal of each *Construct* was not to become an image, but to

exist as a real-time documentation—an intention highlighted by the use of Polaroid film, whose immediacy allowed Kasten to record while further expanding the displacement between light, object, and creator within the work.

A selection of the images alongside the sets themselves, exhibited in the 1980s at John Weber Gallery in New York, presented installations that caught a transitional movement between the photograph and the structure. Fast forward to 2017, and Kasten's exploration of the experiential potential of image continues with the *Progression* series (2017–18). Each is composed of a print where an image that describes colored volumes of fluorescent acrylic accompanied by sculptural shapes of the same acrylic affixed to the surface of the photograph. Creating a conversation between representation and reality, between temporalities—the "then" of the image, and the "now" of the shadow being reflected upon the print—*Progression* hovers between the reflections and shadows that are both inside the image and within our present time.

The use of fluorescent acrylic throughout Kasten's work—a material she has only relatively recently incorporated into her object vocabulary over the last five years—has been incredibly generative for the artist insofar as it has

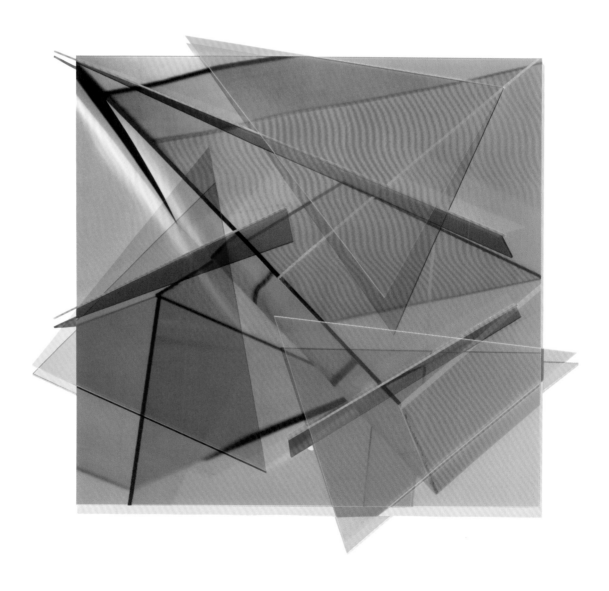

introduced an aspect unique to the material: colored shadows. The way these new kinds of shadows are integrated into Kasten's sculptural practice establishes yet another form for the artist to create space via color. For instance, *Intervention* (2018), an installation created as an extension of the *Artist/City (Crown Hall)* (2018) project, for Hans Ulrich Obrist's Interview Marathons in Chicago.[15] What remains distinctive about this intricate composition is that the neon shadows cast by the acrylic forms become the vehicle that creates an image through light—a sort of opposite methodology to what *Progression* achieves. It is precisely this kind of reversal of logic that most clearly signals Kasten's powers to consistently create something that appears like space itself. What is it that is actually being expressed? Is it a thing? Can it be identified? Can it be considered outside of the correlation between object and representation?

The works are a manifestation of an experience. An atmosphere. A "reinterpretation of the space by being within it, an exchange of the body and environment."[16]

III. Kasten & Barragán

The acknowledgement of the influence architecture has had on Barbara Kasten's path, what the artist describes as "a long-standing interest and relationship with architecture from Le Corbusier and Mies van der Rohe [...] embedded in the structure of her work,"[17] immediately recalls an unintentional dialogue with Luis Barragán.

Barragán is an unlikely figure of comparison if one thinks of Mies's Seagram Building or Le Corbusier's Palace of Assembly, completed respectively in 1958 in New York and 1962 in Chandigarh—though his care for spaces, for contemplation and intimacy, derives from the sublime potential corresponding in Kasten's installations. We can bear in mind the mythology around Barragán's own life; and for that, it is worth considering how both artist and architect operate as creators who deeply believe in the power of experience. Each exercises a sort of doctrine on the haptics of color: an experience so strong and defined that it provokes a tactile sensation.

They share so much. In an exploration that unfolds over many decades, one can see also an unfolding in time. A refusal to follow the rules of a medium

or a discipline—what Barragán termed an "antiacademiscm"—unites their work in an awareness of the power of experience: a profound understanding of color as a phenomenon of light, which forms an active consciousness of the limitations of their collective medium (space).

What remains unaccounted for is their relationship to theater and theatricality—a lived experience that is repeatedly rehearsed through endless, minuscule variations particular to each viewer's experience.[18] The transformational treatment of matter from space into color in Barragán, and from color into space in Kasten, is a long, gentle conversation that has evolved quietly over the years. In the same way that one can have a plastic experience with architecture, in Kasten one can have an architectural experience with plastic media.

This is just one comparative analysis of many that could be made between the works of both. Since for Kasten this dialogue with architecture has been not only fertile, but central to her practice, it is important to displace this dialogue south: to unexpected regions and references. In Kasten's relation to Barragán, this conversation is not about the past, nor happening in the past. This is about a present in which the artist has so dynamically reflected on her breaking of the too-often normative parameters and categories of artistic disciplines—particularly in photography, a medium whose

categorization resists a proper acknowledgment of the multidisciplinary nature of her work. It is within this flexibility and expansiveness that Kasten recognizes herself—where she feels most comfortable, and where, artistically, she thrives.

It is fundamental to be able to inhabit the spaces where one wants to be. As Kasten articulates, this is the progression "to show sculptures that stand alone and are not photographs—for many years, I photographed sculptures and never showed them. Now, I am making real, tridimensional, self-sustaining sculptures—it is like the experience of coming home."[19]

The vibrant, sensorial color composition of Barragán's Casa Gilardi—one of his most important, yet intimate constructions—embraces the life of one family and also the guests they welcome into it. This transformative and improbable gesture finds its power in a singular domestic space. Returning to Kasten's *Intervention,* we encounter an explosion of visual perspectives that create this same emotional architecture. Through this, Kasten imparts on us a gift. Her use of visual, spatial, and experiential resources manifests a space that transmits a sense of intimacy with untamable energy. A sense of fascination in color and space, which is radically hospitable, like Barragán's electrifying residence.

Barbara Kasten in her studio in Chicago, IL, 2020. Courtesy of the artist

[1] Emilio Ambasz, *The Architecture of Luis Barragán* (New York: MoMA, 1976), 123.

[2] Cristina Abellanas Paniagua, "La plástica del color en la obra de Luis Barragán: una aproximación experimental," [The form of color in the work of Luis Barragán: an experimental approach], *Grado en Fundamentos de la Arquitectura* (Valencia: Universitat Politècnica de València, 2015), 26.

[3] Ana Esteban Maluenda, *La arquitectura moderna en Latinoamérica* (Barcelona: Reverte, 2013). Interview with Marie-Pierre Toll originally published in *House & Garden* (New York: 1981).

[4] Aníbal Figueroa Castrejón, *El arte de ver con inocencia: pláticas con Luis Barragán* (Azcapotzalco: Universidad Autonoma Metropolitana, 1989), 114. Translation by the author.

[5] Abellanas Paniagua, "La plástica del color en la obra de Luis Barragán: una aproximación experimental," 26.

[6] Mario G. Schjetnan, "Luis Barragán: The Influential Lyricist of Mexican Culture," *Landscape Architecture Magazine* vol. 72, no. 1 (Washington, DC: American Society of Landscape Architects, 1982), 70–71.

[7] Figueroa Castrejón, *El arte de ver con inocencia: platicas con Luis Barragán*, 114.

[8] In the words of Luis Barragán, "Serenity. Serenity is the great and true antidote against anguish and fear, and today, more than ever, it is the architect's duty to make of it a permanent guest in the home, no matter how sumptuous or how humble. Throughout my work I have always strived to achieve serenity, but one must be on guard not to destroy it by the use of an indiscriminate palette." Schjetnan, "Luis Barragán: The Influential Lyricist of Mexican Culture," 70–71.

[9] Damian Bayon, "An Interview with Luis Barragán," *Landscape Architecture* vol. 66, no. 6 (Washington: American Society of Landscape Architects, 1976), 533.

[10] Schjetnan, "Luis Barragán: The Influential Lyricist of Mexican Culture," 70–71.

[11] Ambasz, *The Architecture of Luis Barragán*, 91.

[12] Leslie Hewitt, "Barbara Kasten," *Bomb Magazine*, no. 131 (2015).

[13] Author interview with Barbara Kasten, Mexico City/Chicago. October 26, 2021.

[14] Barbara Kasten. "Notes and Questions to Myself," *"C" International Photo Magazine*, vol. 7 (London: Ivory Press, 2008), 6.

[15] Hans Ulrich Obrist, "Creative Chicago: An Interview Marathon," September 29, 2018. AON Grand Ballroom, Navy Pier, Chicago, IL.

[16] Author interview October 2021.

[17] Ibid.

[18] Ambasz notes, "Like Borges, Barragán is the author of one archetypal story inexhaustibly reformulated," *The Architecture of Luis Barragán*, 91.

[19] Barbara Kasten, *Sculptural Approaches to Photography: Barbara Kasten*, Talk at the Nasher Sculpture Center, 2019 (11:28–12:00 minutes).

Progression Four (2017), digital
chromogenic print and fluorescent acrylic.
36 × 36 × 7.5 inches (91.44 × 91.44 × 19 cm).
Courtesy of the artist and Bortolami,
New York, NY

Progression Five (2017), digital chromogenic print and fluorescent acrylic. 36 × 36 × 7.5 inches (91.44 × 91.44 × 19 cm). Courtesy of the artist and Bortolami, New York, NY

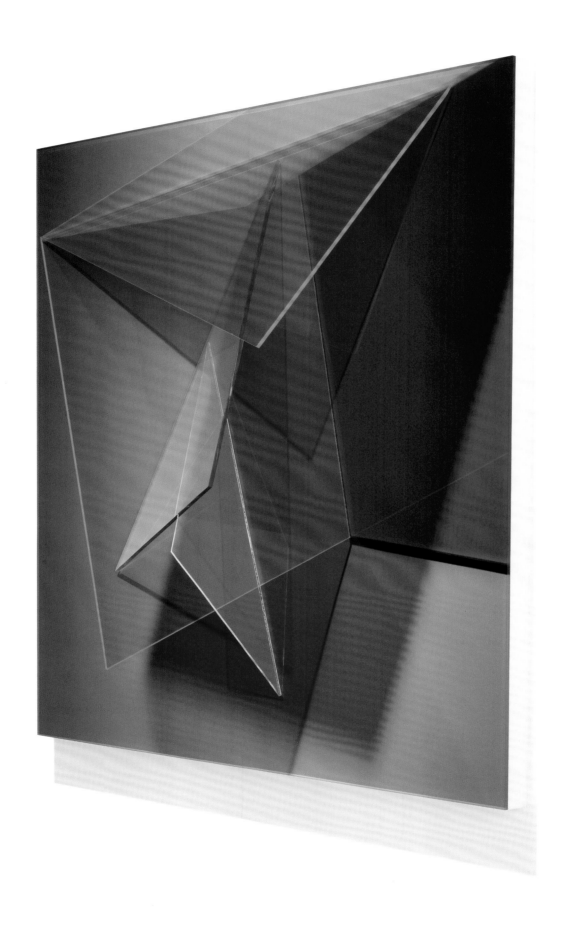

Progression Eight (2018), digital
chromogenic print and fluorescent
acrylic. 36 × 36 × 7.5 inches
(91.44 × 91.44 × 19 cm).
Courtesy of the artist and Bortolami,
New York, NY

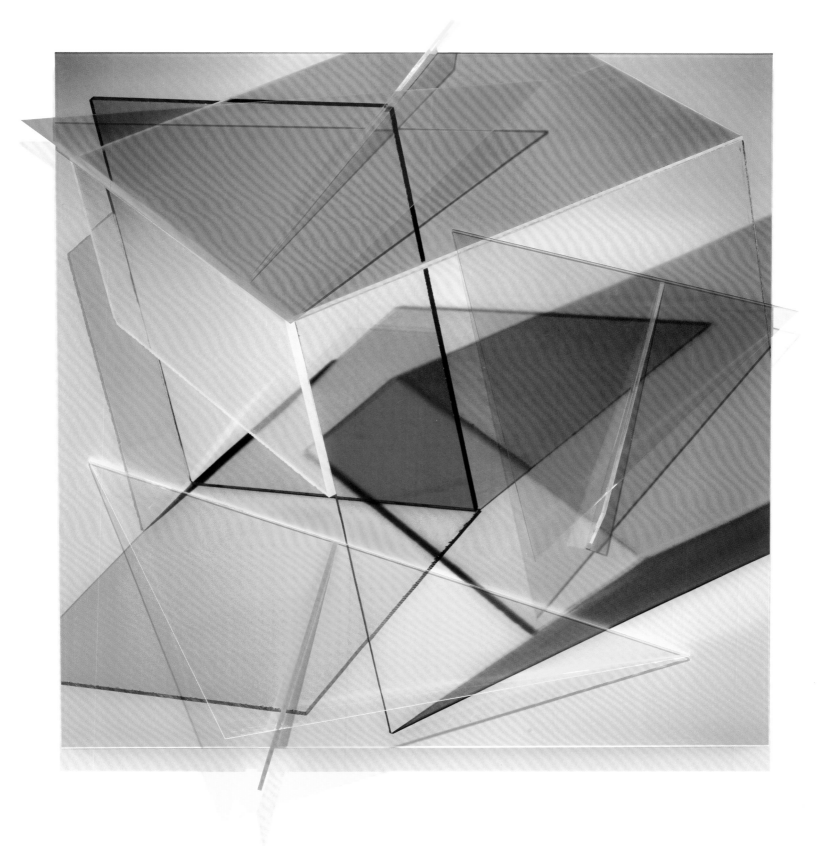

Progression Six (2017), digital chromogenic print and fluorescent acrylic.
36 × 36 × 7.5 inches (91.44 × 91.44 × 19 cm).
Courtesy of the artist and Bortolami,
New York, NY

Progression Nine (2018), digital
chromogenic print and fluorescent
acrylic. 36 × 36 × 7.5 inches
(91.44 × 91.44 × 19 cm).
Courtesy of the artist and Bortolami,
New York, NY

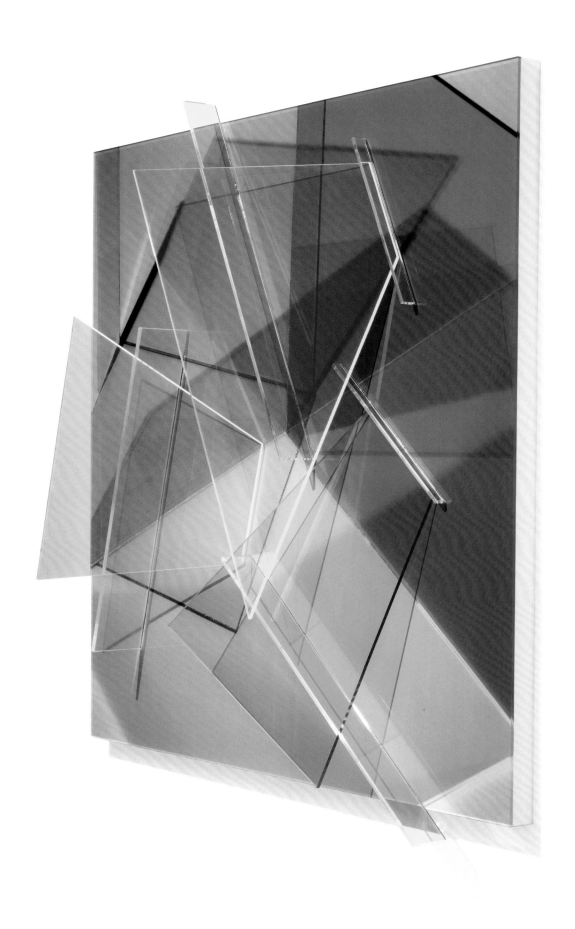

Progression Fifteen (2019), digital chromogenic print and fluorescent acrylic. 48 × 48 × 7.5 inches (121.92 × 121.92 × 19 cm). Photo: Tom Van Eynde. Courtesy of the artist and Bortolami, New York, NY

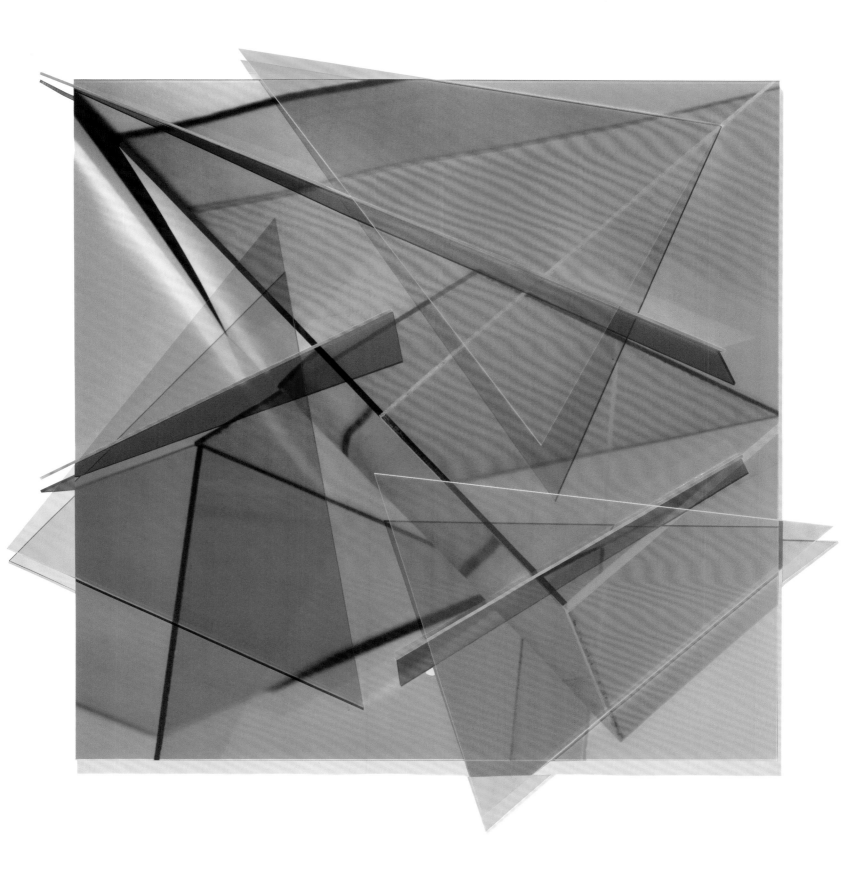

Progression Eleven (2019), digital chromogenic print and fluorescent acrylic. 36 × 36 × 7.5 inches (91.44 × 91.44 × 19 cm). Photo: Tom Van Eynde. Courtesy of the artist and Bortolami, New York, NY

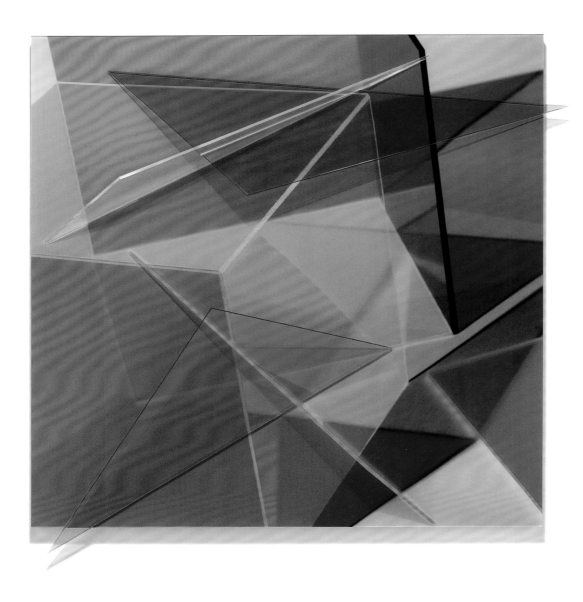

Progression Fourteen (2019),
digital chromogenic print and
fluorescent acrylic. 48 × 48 × 7.5 inches
(121.92 × 121.92 × 19 cm).
Photo: Tom Van Eynde. Courtesy of the
artist and Bortolami, New York, NY

Progression Ten (2019), digital
chromogenic print and fluorescent
acrylic. 36 × 36 × 7.5 inches
(91.44 × 91.44 × 19 cm).
Photo: Tom Van Eynde. Courtesy of the
artist and Bortolami, New York, NY

Progression Twenty-One (2021), digital chromogenic print and fluorescent acrylic. 42 × 42 × 7.5 inches (106.68 × 106.68 × 19 cm). Courtesy of the artist and Thomas Dane Gallery, London, UK

Exhibition History of Individual Works

Axis **(2015)**
HD video (silent, color, 5:20 minutes).
Dimensions variable

Exhibition History
• *Barbara Kasten: Stages*, Institute of
Contemporary Art, University of Pennsylvania,
Philadelphia, PA (2015)

Scenario **(2015)**
Wood, plaster, HD video
(silent, color, 3:38 minutes).
9 × 12 × 18 feet (2.74 × 3.65 × 5.48 m)

Exhibition History
• *Barbara Kasten: Stages*, Graham Foundation,
Chicago, IL (2015)
• *Barbara Kasten: Scenarios*, Aspen Art
Museum, Aspen, CO (2020–21)

Sideways **(2015/2020)**
HD video (silent, color, 3:30 minutes).
Dimensions variable

Exhibition History
• *SET MOTION*, Bortolami, New York, NY (2015)
• *Barbara Kasten: Scenarios*, Aspen Art
Museum, Aspen, CO (2020–21)

Sideways Corner **(2016)**
HD video (silent, color, 8:19 minutes).
Dimensions variable

Exhibition History
• *Barbara Kasten: Staging Architecture*, Kadel
Willborn Gallery, Düsseldorf, Germany (2016)
• *Barbara Kasten: Stages*, MOCA Pacific Design
Center, Los Angeles, CA (2016)
• *Barbara Kasten: Sideways Corner*, Soluna
Festival, Morton H Meyerson Symphony Center,
Dallas, TX (2016)
• *Barbara Kasten: WORKS*, Kunstmuseum
Wolfsburg, Wolfsburg, Germany (2020)

Parallels **(2017)**
Fluorescent acrylic.
32 × 98 × 96 inches (81.5 × 249 × 244 cm)

Exhibition History
• *Barbara Kasten: Parti Pris*, Bortolami,
New York, NY (2017)
• *Barbara Kasten: Parallels*, Sammlung
Philara, Düsseldorf, Germany (2018)
• *Barbara Kasten: Scenarios*, Aspen Art
Museum, Aspen, CO,(2020–21)

Revolutions **(2017/2022)**
Paper, HD video (silent, color,
3:47 minutes). Dimensions variable.

Exhibition History
• *Barbara Kasten: Intervals*, Thomas Dane
Gallery, London, UK (2017)
• *Barbara Kasten*, Sammlung Goetz, Munich,
Germany (2022)

Crossover **(2020)**
Fluorescent acrylic, paper, HD video (color,
silent, 5:51 minutes).
Dimensions variable

Exhibition History
• *Less is a Bore*, K10, Arthena Foundation,
Düsseldorf, Germany (2016)
• *Words at an Exhibition* 《열 장의 이야기와 다섯 편의
시》 *an exhibition in ten chapters and five
poems*, Busan Biennale, Busan, South Korea
(2020)
• *Barbara Kasten: Scenarios*, Aspen Art
Museum, Aspen, CO (2020–21)

Barbara Kasten during the installation
of *Artist/City* (*Crown Hall*) (2018).
Photo: Stephanie Cristello.
Courtesy of the author

Acknowledgements

With sincerest gratitude to the dedicated team whose work went into making this book possible, thank you. To authors Hans Ulrich Obrist, Humberto Moro, and Mimi Zeiger, I am honored to collaborate with you and your brilliant insights into Barbara Kasten's recent work—your writing has provided a critical voice in understanding this chapter of her practice in the context of a long career, with keen examination into the concepts that fuel these site-specific installations. We are grateful to Edoardo Ghizzoni of Skira for so enthusiastically welcoming this concept, and to Anna Cattaneo, Emma Cavazzini, Andrew Ellis, and Paola Ranzini Pallavicini, for their contributions on behalf of the publisher.

I would also like to thank Sarah Herda and James Pike of the Graham Foundation, whose commitment and guidance to the early stages of the project following the award of the 2020 grant allowed for essential research to frame the premise of this publication; the support of Eva Silverman at the Terra Foundation for American Art for their help in conceptualizing programming surrounding this book as part of Art Design Chicago; Rachel Adams of the Bemis Center for Contemporary Arts for supporting my residency to develop the focus and list of authors; Nicola Lees and Max Weintraub of the Aspen Art Museum for presenting *Barbara Kasten: Scenarios* in a most challenging year; the IIT College of Architecture for their support of *Artist/City (Crown Hall)* in 2018; the grant of the Illinois Arts Council; and Dan Handel and Tal Erez of Manifest Institute for the program associated with this book in June of 2022.

This publication would not have been achieved without the unwavering support of Stefania Bortolami and the numerous rewarding conversations had over travel to view these exhibitions with Claire Bergeal of Bortolami Gallery in New York, Iris Kadel and Moritz Willborn of Kadel Willborn Gallery in Düsseldorf, Hannah Hoffman of Hannah Hoffman Gallery in Los Angeles, and Tom Dingle of Thomas Dane Gallery in London. We look forward to an exhibition informed by this book in Fall of 2022 through Sibylle Friche and Aron Gent of DOCUMENT in Chicago.

The groundwork for this book was incited by the rigor and dedication of Alex Klein at the Institute of Contemporary Art at the University of Pennsylvania in Philadelphia—thank you for all you have done to concretize Kasten's life and work within the cannon of contemporary art. From the artist's studio, Lauren McPhillips and Kate Bowen have been integral to the realization of these ambitious projects. To my editor, Joel Kuennen, your support, clarity, and generosity is simply beyond words.

Finally—Barbara, it is hard to measure the admiration we all possess for you and your work. Your practice, an emblem of tenacity, ingenuity, and steadfast determination, is an absolute inspiration. Your profound friendship and working so closely with you, amid the many challenges and fears presented in the lead up to this publication, is one of the greatest joys I have had the pleasure being a part of.

Thank you.

Stephanie Cristello